Imagining Paradise
New and Selected Poems

Imagining Paradise
New and Selected Poems

Barry Gifford

Seven Stories Press
New York

ACKNOWLEDGMENTS: Some of these poems have previously appeared in the following publications: *Alcaeus Review, Artisans Almanak, American Poets Say Goodbye to the Twentieth Century, Arx, Aux Arcs, The Baltimore Sun, Beat Scene Press Chapbooks, Beloit Poetry Journal, The Berkeley Monthly, Big River News, Blackberry Books, Blue Fife, Booglit, Bordertown* (Chronicle Books), *Calafia: The California Poetry Anthology* (Y'Bird Books), *California Quarterly, Chicago Review, Christopher's Books Famous Authors Calendar, Cimarron Review, A Marshall Clements/David Stivender Christmas Card, Cranium Press Broadsides, Cuadrilátero* (Madrid), *Donald S. Ellis Chapbooks, Esquire, Exquisite Corpse, Fandango* (Rome), *First Intensity* (Lawrence, Kansas), *Florida Quarterly, A George Hall Broadside, HandBook, Handshake Editions* (Paris), *Homage To The Chinese Masters* (Bejing), *Hormone Derange Editions, Jacket* (Sydney), *Journal 31, Kuksu, Lampeter Muse, Madame Class* (Milan), *The Madison Review, Madrugada, Rain, Measure, Mendocino Beacon, Poésie* (Paris), *The New Yorker, The Niagara Magazine, Northern Lights* (London), *La Nouvelle Revue Française* (Paris), *Painted Bride Quarterly, Panta* (Milan), *Poetry Flash, Poetry Japan, Quiksilver, Road Apple Review, Romania Literara* (Bucharest), *Shaman Drum Broadside Number One, Shenandoah, Sonoma State Poetry Festival Program, South Florida Poetry Journal, Sparks of Fire, Sumus, Tarpaulin Sky, Titmouse Review, Transit* (U.K.), *Tribal Village* (Toronto), *Truck, Twelfth Key, Twigs, Volta* (Los Angeles), *Western American Literature, White Pine, Will* (Tokyo), *Wisconsin Review,* and *Wood Ibis.*

"The Last Words of Arthur Rimbaud" was published in a limited edition by The Bancroft Library Press (University of California, Berkeley, 1998).

"Hey, Ludwig, Grab Yourself a Pigfoot" was published in the anthology *Best Music Writing 2009,* edited by Greil Marcus and Daphne Carr (Da Capo Press).

The author wishes to express his gratitude to Joyce Jenkins and Dan Simon for their editorial expertise, as well as their thoughtful and patient work in the preparation of this book.

Book design by Jon Gilbert

Library of Congress Cataloging-in-Publication Data

Gifford, Barry, 1946-
Imagining paradise : new and selected poems / Barry Gifford. — A Seven Stories Press 1st ed.
     p. cm.
ISBN 978-1-60980-374-2
I. Title.
PS3557.I283144 2012
811'.54—dc23

                                    2011042451

Printed in the USA.

9 8 7 6 5 4 3 2 1

Contents

SELECTED POEMS 1967–2006

The Blood of the Parade (1967)   9
Coyote Tantras (1973)   13
Flaubert at Key West (1997)   22
Replies to Wang Wei (2001)   103
    The Life of Wang Wei by Chang Chiu-ling   103
    Persimmons: Poems for Paintings   111
    Poems From Snail Hut   161
    Horse hauling timber out of Hokkaido forest   167
The Last Words of Arthur Rimbaud (2004)   180
As If It Were a Photograph (2004)   184
Shooting Pool in the Dark (2004)   203
Back in America (2004)   218
Las cuatro reinas/The Four Queens (2006)   240

IMAGINING PARADISE: NEW POEMS   295

BIBLIOGRAPHY   345
INDEX OF TITLES AND FIRST LINES   346

Selected Poems

1967–2006

The Blood of the Parade
(1967)

Poem

Silence, silence
croak the old men
spit in the shave-cup
coal-black eyes
      in the drain

The Old Boy

Sitting alone
on your lined
floor moving
your miniature men
alone

and at school
they have told you
how it will be

that you will be
alone
holding yourself
in the dark

and you
you do enjoy
it that way
alone

you have made
your lips
moist in
front of them

and they have
put you away for
that and
still

you do it
still
where you are
alone

you hold yourself
tighter and have
let your nails
grow long

you have
shown yourself
what it is
to be a man
alone

let them
open the door
once   once more
and give them
your manhood

here is the
knife they
have left you

they have left
it here
for you to cut with

go ahead
cut it off
they have left
it here for you

slip it
under the door

so they
will test
it first
and hold it
in the water

and when they
let you out

go away
to the hills
where

you can
live
with the
frogs

and
be the boy
you have
always loved

Coyote Tantras
(1973)

XV

for Paul

At Point Lobos

smell of wolf
rolls across the water
Coyote takes to trail

One lone vision
remains

lurks along

the

pebbld dark

steely clever

XXXVII

Plea to Coyote For Mankind

My Friend Coyote,

   silent mover
      who threatens the world
      with earthquakes
         & thunderstorms
      while giving birth
         to children
     & the dawn,

is my vision & being

     I am Coyote
as he is the stars &
     I am the sun

We live in the shadow & song of Coyote
   and die in the winter of the wolf

Coyote is the constant visitor & reminder
   of the open road to everywhere

     with Buddhalike awareness he
     prowls thru backwoods of the
     universe, steady,
            skipping unnoticed

& solitary over the planet,
gathering seeds from the surface of the center

of the Void,

planting, restless, rejected,

bound-in-balance

configuration of outlook & experience, noblest
of all medicine men, witchdoctors and shamans,
priests & hobos,

upholder of the magic rituals
of life,
created, seized and driven by
Nature

Speaks-Only-The-Truth,
Follows-No-Crooked-Trails,
my blessings & prayers to you,
King Coyote,
may you trample the hatred & lies of this life,

& MAKE MEN FREE

LXXXVIII

Coyote did not know how to swim.
"What is this language Poets use?"
he asked.
Coyote went hungry until he learned
how to fish.
By the time spring came Coyote was thin.
"What kind of wind blows crooked?"
he asked.
When Bear laughed he farted.
Coyote blew his nose on a leaf.
"What kind of God inhabits a stone?"
he asked.
Geese flew past the mountain,
turning North.
Coyote turned over a rock
in his mind.
"Let's see what words are left,"
he said.

XCIX

Hunters in the Kootenays

       after black bear,

   saw a string of coyotes

     a mile long

  Sun shot holes in them
(They were carrying gold to the mountains

  The hunters went blind,
and tried to crawl
back down on their
    hands and knees
When their sight returned, they lookd
    for the coyotes

    The trail was empty.

   (What became of Coyote

   was Nothing

CI

Coyote stood by the river

with his lady,
where
the North Alouette
spills into the Fraser

"Write down what you see,"

said Coyote,

"just that—
"anything else

is your own fault"

CII

Coyote sat
    on a slope
above a wire corral
    on the plains,
a whitefaced sorrel
ran along the Alouette
    chasing crows

"What a racket"
yawned Coyote, nudging
    nearer the sun

  "All this room
        on
          one great star—

            Who can speak?"

CXVI

for Duane Big Eagle

Coyote traversed
      the Great White Mountains,
      and came upon an Old Man
      a-lean a tall pine
      by a pool

"Who are you?" Coyote asked the man

"The Great White One," he said, without looking up
"And who may young First-to-speak be?"

"Coyotl-No-Fool," said Coyote, grinning proudly
"What do you do here so far from others?"

The Old Man laughed,

      "I grow my white hair thirty feet long,
bathe under waterfalls three thousand feet high,
empty one thousand jugsful of wine when I want!"

Coyote was stunned

The Old Man did not look up, but laughed again and again

      "Call me High Plains Dragon Master, call me
Green Lotus Man, call me
      'Old Wine Genius' ha ha ha ha ha"

Coyote took off fast—

Li-Po did not look up, but waved Coyote

      swift departure

CXVII

Li-Po and Coyote lay drunk
    in the blue snow
Passersby sneered at them,
    and hurried past
    Only one old bum
stopped to see
what was left
in their bottle,
    swigged the final drop
    and himself collapsed
nearby.

    "Ah Coyote," mumbled Li-Po,

        "Only the great drinkers

    have left us their names"

Flaubert at Key West
(1997)

Maria La O

In 1959, my cousin Chris and I
accompanied my Uncle Les
from Tampa to Jacksonville,
where he had business to do.
I was twelve, Chris sixteen.
Jacksonville was a small town
then, palms lined the street
where I bought a papaya drink
from a sidewalk stand.
We ate lunch in a big hotel.
I watched people through
a long, plate-glass window
behind our booth. After lunch,
Uncle Les passed out Havanas.
We lit them and puffed away
as the three of us left the hotel
and strolled down the street.
Passersby stared at me, a small boy
smoking a big, black, Cuban cigar.
I loved the taste of it, bitter

after eating sweet *flan*
for dessert, and breathed deeply
the romantic aroma of smoke
and tropical air. Thirty-five
years later I recall the smell,
the blue sailfish shirt
I wore, the Florida that
isn't there any more.

Nine May Ninety-six

The matador Luis Miguel Dominguín
died yesterday at sixty-nine in Cadiz
He was a show-off, kissed the bulls
before killing them, called himself Numero Uno
No great shakes with a cape,
he was masterful with the banderillas
Another supreme egotist, Ernest Hemingway,
preferred Antonio Ordoñez, he said,
but Hemingway was clearly envious of Luis
and, I believe, a dishonest reporter
Famous cocksman, Dominguín caroused
with Ava Gardner and other actresses,
one of whom, Lucía Bosé, he married
He was a friend of my great-aunt Madeleine's
and when I was twelve he sent me
an autographed black and white picture
of himself making a pass with a bull
Years later, we shared a girlfriend
I still have the photo in a cigar box
The girl is long gone, of course,
but I thought about her this morning
when I read Dominguín's obituary
in the New Orleans Times-Picayune
She had a beautiful laugh
I wonder if Dominguín remembered that.

Música Latina

In Barcelona
for the first time
gray March
I think of my friend
Richard Matas
half-French
half-Catalán
poet
hanged himself
in a hotel room
on Ramblas
by the
port
I remember
his tall
lovely
daughter
20 when
he died
My one true love
Richard said
in his last note
By taking
his own
life
he missed
hers

Maracas

Lorca at the
Hotel Venus
1930
Santiago
de Cuba
boys rattle
as they
walk

A Few Words about Rimbaud

A hundred and eleven
           years ago
Rimbaud was in
               Abyssinia
      land of men
        with tails
             striped faces
   running guns
      slaves, coffee
   from Tadjoura
           or Djibouti
      to Harar
      and beyond
         the first white man
              to go south
  sees nothing
        to write about
         bored by
              the desert
      but can't
                give it
                up
professional bad boy
   confused
        fucked over
            by savages
     words puny
        in the face
             of Africa

Arthur!
were you
satisfied
with
this
punishment?

Epiphany for Gérald Neveu

A truck hauling a palm tree
through the Luxembourg Gardens
Dozens of pretty girls, as always
A few classic bums dozing
against the museum wall
Soon-no-longer-young men reading
magazines, feigning disinterest
sneaking peeks from corners of their eye
The apartment at the top of the building
on the corner of the Avenue de l'Observatoire
reigns over the park like a mountain peak
I've wanted to live there ever since
I first saw it twenty-five years ago
Today I imagine a faded beauty
wearing only a leopard skin brassiere
and jewel-rimmed dark glasses
looking down on us, surveying her domain
through a powerful telescope
Sudden squeals of schoolgirls
trading photographs under the branches
alert the drowsers in wire chairs
The sky is no longer dead
My most understanding readers
as well as yours
have yet to be born

Pseudo-Pindaric Ode to Francis Jammes

Of course, Jammes was mad.
His reality was his imagination—
it was there he lived and made love
with flowers, bees, trees, perfect virgins.
The Catholic was a Pan-theist,
a magnificent, graceful dreamer.
O so dementedly delicate to encrust
a lofty oak with a rill of sunburst bees!
The naked girl was his Rima, trembling
like a wild quince blossom in the rain,
the refuge of the poet ablaze with
Stars-of-China, soft feathers of fog,
the chill of a rainbow.
What have men done to make you suffer so?
asks the girl, To make your soul bleed?
They have lied! shrieks the poet.
Sometimes I've wanted to go far away
to some wild shore with my dogs, where
one sees only the sun and the water
rising and falling to die entwined.
This is the point of madness, as she says,
and Jammes makes it elegantly.

Highway 83

In Zapata, Texas
I saw a Mexican
girl
driving an
old Dodge pickup
She was so beautiful
for one moment
the earth
stopped spinning
and everything that
ever
happened
to me
made perfect
sense

Vision del Calle Cruz Rey

Old man
    sitting in his
        yard
    in Caseta
under the only
            tree
        reading
            Dostoevsky's
            Los Diablos
skinny dog
    circling
        him
            slowly

Whores in the Club Papagayo

Under dim
 red
   light
purposeful reptiles
    slide
  from muddy
   banks
  into green
slimy water

Poem Ut Animum Nostrum Purget

She lov'd Villon—
    I was a poet, but
    no Villon;

She lov'd Scarlatti—
    I made music, but
    most unlike Scarlatti;

She lov'd Renoir—
    and I did not paint.

My Father

The day
he died

Pops, my mother's father, sat
in the kitchen

drinking
tea,

toast crumbs
in his lap,

crying.
Death's

boy, I looked out

the livingroom
window

for the big
blue car.

In Sight

Rain splinters the bridge
across from the Burma
Road Bar & Grill
where I sit drinking
beer and watching
the waitress.
There isn't much
curve to her body
I like her hands
deliberate but tender.
Her face is
ordinary. What really attracts me
are her eyes
the colorless
quality they reflect
opaque absorption
of neglect.

How Many Mangos in
Mango Chutney

There is a broken heart
in the Chinese restaurant
sitting at a booth
with a low-tugged hat
and its eyes are on the coatrack
All night it has been telling me
to order a big meal
and get on with my soup
but I muff it
I lose the fly ball in the sun
I pull my hat lower in the booth
The sun has killed my chance of a dark day
Whoever is running on the beach
will never get to know me
There is music here
There is romance
At the crack of a bat
the shortstop breaks to his left
All of the ears in the Chinese restaurant
are not able to follow the sound
The lady with the long hands
and rouge fingernails is eyeing me
I might have known

Larry

My mother
had a husband
who was
crazy, she said.

He refused
to get up,
like Bartleby.

That's not so
crazy, I said;
look at it this way:

The way the world is
men never really know
what it's like to die

until it's too late
and then they
don't want to.

He wasn't crazy, Ma, that's
too easy
to say.

He must have been looking
a long time
to have thought

he lost it
in his bed, not
his head.

Paris Street

Wind up gray
schoolgirl's skirt—
As she passed
copper ringlets
touched my shoulder.
Seven years later,
agonizing over
her little blue cap!

North Beach Chinese Sonnet

Chinese children chase pigeons,
  fish swirl
  in ponds
at evening—

I think
of my four day-dead cat
that was such a beauty,
all black with a touch
of white on her belly—

Nothing is more unbelievable
than death, —
I keep looking around
for what's
not there.

Watching Fish

Watching
fish
swim
in
a
Chinatown
window

five
old
men
in
hats

The Season of Truth

This is valuable experience,
lying in bed with the window open
on a cold, late October morning.
My father might not have understood it
but I have written some of my best poems
this way. Sunlight streams across the floor,
reminding me of my room at the back
of the house in Chicago.
It was always cold in there,
I liked it. I could scrape my name
in the ice on the window glass with my fingernail.
It was nicest when the sun shone on the snow
not hot enough to melt it,
but that was rare, usually the sky was gray,
and made me want to get away.
Born in Vienna, my father chose Chicago
to die in. Pigeons pecking in gutters,
frozen overcoats at bus stops.
The coast air is clear, I am happy here.
Chicago comes closest late in the afternoon,
when days are short. Winter, rain,
are more real than the rest. In truth,
that is when I am most relaxed and feel best.

At the Albright-Knox

for Ray Neinstein

Pollock's painting
"Cotton Pickers"
done in 1939
impressed me more than anything else
in the entire museum
including his own later work.
Somehow I felt more certain
of myself, more certain
the bad Rousseau still-life
hanging downstairs
was really bad
or at least uninteresting,
that Seurat really is my favorite painter,
that Milton Avery's yellow cow
is as possible as almost anything,
& that when she was young
my mother had the longest,
most beautiful auburn hair
in America.

Sonnet to a Marble Beauty

O silent love
so many years
you've stood & dreamed alone
how fair remained
& yet unstained,
how tender despite stone.
Twenty years I've known you now,
(I wonder do you still remember)
when I was ten
I kissed your cheek
(it was a similar December)
& pressed my own upon it,
today my fingers trace your lips,
caress your plain white bonnet.

Cino

O beauties
   I loved!
you knew nothing of me,
of my art, save its lure—
Admirers of passion,
the dare, of strength,
not heart, what's pure,
thus we parted, at length.
Lips, words, dreams,
thou jewels of lust,
I have had enough of women—
such is this troubador's disgust.

Bohemian Cigar Store, San Francisco

Last week
I was 28

Rumpled-pants Pete
plays pinball

Sicilian cardsharps
in hats

One Sunday
when Domenico

and Rosa
owned the place

old men
wrinkled eyes

blazing like
Corsican suns

handed my
daughter around

the bar
mumbling 'bella, bella'

Letter to Proust No. 2

Dear M.,
How I see the bee this morning
Is how D.H. Lawrence must have seen
Most things—insidious, buzzing, a threat.
That that Lawrence suspicioned is evident today—
I doubt that anyone could live much past forty
With such an attitude.
Lawrence's beard was a stationary replica
Of this kind of fear. He substituted the general fear
Of the mind for the specific fear of the mines—
There was the pansy, yes, but there was also the bee.
Very much the bee, invading the pansy, sucking it out—
That's how Lawrence saw it.
The fly is attracted to base secretions, sweat and shit—
'Twas the flower's smell seduced D.H., the basis of beauty;
He spent his life trying to find a way to protect it.
There is no way to conceal oneself from the bee.
One has only to sit and let it touch, choose, sting
Or be gone; any immunity is temporary.
The bee-shark cruises in the August grass, goldly, blackly,
Testing various strengths; assumption without thought;
        sustenance.

Letter to Proust No. 5

Dear Marcel,
It is another hot day here.
I sit at the zenith of the stone steps and stare out
At the whiteness of the water.
From this proximity the horizon appears
An irregular and thin black line,
A lone interrupter of the Corsican sun.
Lawrence claims the effect in Sardinia
As similar as the ripeness of olives
In the cold wash of a mountain stream.
A woman with a basket on her head spouts brandied cherries
From her mouth; the woman is black, her lover a dark
    Norway Blue.
The sun's only yellow in Sardinia.
From this place to yours appears an unbroken
Path of burnt sienna leaves.
How strange the weak comparison; it is the way
The sun leaves you.
The sun eats through the burial mounds on the hills,
Fastening bones to the earth.
There are no birds in this immense sky.
With a handful of paint I could cover the sun.

Denver Alba

Awakened in Denver
honking cars out hotel window
drizzly railyards
    Baudelaire
  at dawn
listening to his mistress's
    stomach rumble

Poem

My arm
around
  your small
    waist

suddenly reminded
of rain
    red maple
      trees
    at Kyoto

After Yosano Akiko

Coming from your bed
into the cold dawn
I picture you
still curled
under the covers
and do not mind
the snowflakes settling
on my hair.

Lives of the French
Impressionist Painters

MONET

Monet had a beautiful garden that
nobody took care of after his death.
He dreamed there were crocodiles in
his lily pond but didn't tell anyone
even though he continued to look for
them there. "I always try to tell a
story," he told those who asked. He
constantly forgot what he was going
to say. Late one night he dropped his
spectacles into the pond. Monet fell
asleep on a bench in his garden and
was devoured by a red tiger.

PISSARRO AND CÉZANNE

Here they are in a field about 1890.
Two bearded men with hats on, one
with a stick. It's Pissarro. It looks as if
he is speaking and Cézanne's eyes are
very expressive though we can't really
see them. Cézanne wears a smock,
Pissarro a jacket, boots, a pack on his
back. Cézanne is the more famous of
the two, he still is. He admires
Pissarro's paintings of Rouen. "You
have a way with churches," he has
told him. Camille has a wonderful

white beard, Paul a wonderful brown
one. They are surrounded by flowers,
a field of flowers, their hats pulled
low. There are colors everywhere.

MANET

In the summer of 1874, Monet,
Renoir and Manet were together at
Argenteuil. They painted portraits of
one another and their wives and
boats. Manet fainted and fell off the
pier into the water. Renoir fished him
out but Monet pushed him back in.
Renoir pushed Monet in. Manet
drowned, Monet splashed about,
Renoir stood on the pier pointing and
laughing.

DEGAS

Hated landscapes. Liked women.
Refused to be influenced, he said.
Kept his hat on. Never forgave Renoir
for not inviting him to Argenteuil.
Insulted Gauguin. Gray water in the
gutters. Painted boats. Never visited
Japan. Found orange.

PISSARRO

Friendships broke down. He lived into
the twentieth century with a wonderful
beard. "*Il n'y a que la peinture qui
compte.*" Pissarro was a professional
and he always knew it. "*Il n'y a que la
peinture qui compte.*" He had three sons,
Lucien, Rodo and Felix. Rodo had a
beard and looked like a rabbi, Lucien
a dandy, Felix a student. Pissarro paid
them little attention.

RENOIR

He was happiest with the painting of
his daughter. She was a perfect
subject. In the evenings he strolled
about with a yellow parrot on his
sleeve. He could make the parrot
disappear then reappear a different
color. The Paris street boys followed
him and begged him to do the trick.
He pretended not to remember
pushing Monet into the water at
Argenteuil. Renoir scolded his
daughter for painting a rose green.

SEURAT

When he was a little boy Seurat lost
his favorite blue cap. Thunderstorms
fascinated him. He drew the figure of
a horse and erased it. The Seine
looked thick and black but it never
stayed that way. Seurat was not much
of a dancer. "I prefer the company of
light," he told a friend's wife. There
were seldom any mountains. In 1879
he wrote: "After all, it is the wind
that is imperfect."

MORISOT

Manet was her brother-in-law. Valéry
drank coffee in the kitchen. She could
see how confusing it was through the
window. Kept the Orient in the
cabinet but used it freely. Morisot
standing in a shallow blue pool with
her clothes on and a small white and
gold dog. Collected lamps. She was
secretly afraid she'd swallowed objects
she'd misplaced.

CÉZANNE

Apricots and peaches. He never drove
a silver car. Cézanne could paint the
sound of a dropping chestnut. He was
a polite hermit in his later years
though once on holiday in Morocco
bought a Turk's ear in a bazaar.
Cézanne loved fish.

GAUGUIN

Gauguin was very proud of his nose.
A genuine admirer of Pissarro, who
sent pressed roses to Tahiti. Gauguin
was uncomfortable everywhere except
on October Saturdays in Illinois. Slept
fully clothed. Had a recurring dream
about stepping on white snakes in the
desert. Long voyages depressed him,
he couldn't paint for weeks afterward.
After Gauguin's death his final
mistress told reporters he was a
skillful lover but admitted her distaste
for anal intercourse.

CASSATT

She preferred large men. Cassatt had
the provincial's unreasonable affection
for Paris and would frequently bore
her listeners with descriptions of
Philadelphia on rainy Sunday
afternoons. Wrote several novels
dealing with unrequited love which
she burned. Brought an orange to
Degas each time she visited him at his
studio. "My dear Cassatt," he once
telegrammed from Rome, "I am in
need of tender grey."

SISLEY

An inveterate borrower. Always wore
an overcoat. Sisley tried to imagine
how birds hid from one another. He
was convinced they could change
color. Took long walks. His idol was
Wild Bill Hickock and his dream was
to shoot out the lights along the
Champs Élysées. Took in stray cats.
A man of simple tastes he pretended
his enemies had died.

At an Exhibition of Scrolls & Drawings by Tomioka Tessai: 2nd December 1968

Old Tessai
Old Tomioka
            Ancient Painter Sage
      with eyes & beard of Ho Chi Minh
      Berobed and bemused, pearld
      & glittered grin

                  Old Hero of Kyoto
            Nanga Prophet
                  Sweet being of the old capital
            gentle man
                  Life-essence scattered
      on tattered bamboo rug
            piles of books   landscape drawings
      kettles & Baskets beweaved and beworn
                  Old glaring Forever-cast eyes
            seen thru centuries & filled,
            like brow of Gurdjieff,
      with Holy Gift of Seeing

      Tea burns in flower vase
      The walls of your room shine
      Your face a character burnt in wood

   Bundles of sticks
            bamboo threads for morning fire

            P'eng-Lai

the mount balled above the village
wound like yarn thru the sky

What Father of Occidental Medicine
have you drawn? What alchemist with
drooping nails & Cyrano nose?

Basho on horseback
                simple hills
                ragged children
        Issa hiding in the weeds?
The stream is Shiki
                grassblown blend of colors
purple reeds for Poets

        Ah! Here!
        the recluse! the eccentric!
The opium smoker, the scholar, the warrior
        the painter, the lover
                Han Shans & Shih-tes
            Mifunes & Sesshus
        sandaled & stoned
                Koto, pipe and scroll
bells ringing

Flowers
Red foliage at the Eigenji
        1869 scroll   trees
                seen now as
                telephone
                poles

Closer
                    trees are red
              drop leaves
                past bridge
        Two men hid in shrubs
        Bonsai fluff above ricefields
        Boats drift past spotted cliffs

              Your Eye,
                so tender & so right

                    Here blowfish
              lobster & frog
          crab & clam marked for wall

              Your legend,
                waltzing in the sea

Tsukigase's inlets
        jagged cliff briars & snow

        High cliff with face of an eagle
          Shangri-La devoured by clouds
                    yawning rocks
                      & rapids
          Boatmen
                    Fishermen sculpted for scroll
              reveal with hands
              what Poet dreams

              Up cliffside
          Hard trail

to scale

A torch
        a shining starry eyeglass temple
aglow in boulder
                a tired footbridge
                led to hidden abode
                of Mi Fu

Sumos & Patriarchs
        the same dull mouths
                chinbone &
                sloed eye

Autumn fan clearing over Higashiyama
shields sleeping Buddha from bamboo rain

        Pine & Fungus: Integrity
                & Firmness
                        (How drab that gray
                        rose amidst the pine)
"Abundant good fortune, great longevity,
a multitude of sons"

Mochi-pounders next to Ming-Ts'an, Zen Master
eating potatoes: his teeth are falling out; he's bald;
his lids droop badly on the sides: eyeballs Sanpaku
        Does he sing & dance?
Merchants and books and skyhouse retreats
Gluttony
        Drunkenness
                Greed

But this Final Spirit
The Gay One, Fu Lu Shou
God Of Happiness
peeping blue duckegg eyes
bluebird eyes
with snowy brows &
blowing beard
What songs he purred
that so few heard
A gentler Saint cannot be

My blessings to You, O Holy,
I bow in loving Grace

Tung-Po brews tea
while his wife cooks
Autumn sweeps trees clean
as Huai-Su scrawls on banana leaf

Fuji reigns on Tiger's fang
lava groans for springtime

Ruriko's Buddha-finger
lingers drowsily
in rain
Kuan-Yin awaits
Nothingness on a stone
in the moon

Lu T'ung
a wealthy man, sampling tea

Would he slay the servants if he didn't like it?

A lake at Hangchow
    slithers thru
  rocks
        Su Tung-P'o pats his stomach
      The apricots blossom

                The snail-hut of Chao-Hsien
                glints gold in frost

                Seaweed still gathered
                from the sea

    Noble Tessai,
                guide of A Journey In Fancy
                To The Realm Of Immortals,

                your diamond peaks
                are jewels of distant
                        song

Chinese Notes

Separated by a river
I try not to think of you
At least my tears
please the flowers.

•

Startled by a bird
I clutch my heart
as if you'd flown
out from it.

•

Rainy, windy,
poor footing,
Barely seen
the river boat light.

•

Snow fills
the cat's
footprints.

•

Ah, the stars
Ten thousand
silver horses.

•

Not much further
to her door
my horse's head
bent against
the flying snow
Fortunately, he knows
the way.

•

I saw her once
on the blue riverbank
the whitest face
and hands
a courtesan
on a rare
outing.

●

There is a full moon
Going to meet a new friend
I am assailed by ghosts
of fury and disappointment
I hope my face
will not betray me.

●

We passed one afternoon
in pleasant conversation
before parting
she to the East
I to remain
How differently
I would have behaved
had I known
our separation
would be for ever.

●

In the distant mountains
a solitary traveler
on horseback
picks his way carefully
along a rock-strewn path
Suddenly black clouds
devour the sun
A ferocious storm
forces him
to take shelter
under a close-by ledge
Watching the rain
he amuses himself
with thoughts of
former mistresses
and his children.

•

Butterfly lands
on book
I wait and wait
to turn the page
studying light
through wings
green, orange,
yellow, pink.

•

Red fish
circling in
shallow water
Two young girls
laughing, shaking
their wet hair

●

From my sickbed
bird screeches
are faint
and I no longer
care about the moon

●

Sparrows pick
at gravel
windy fog
That day
you left
was like this
no warmth
or form;
hopeless.

●

Lately my dreams
reveal little
of interest
no lust or envy
only boats
or horses.

•

Hazy hills
heavy sun
no birds
Unpleasant weather
leaves undisturbed
only new lovers.

•

Far from family
and friends
hiking in
unfamiliar woods
the past
unfolds as on
a Chinese screen
This sky
full of waves
faces glimpsed
in dreams
ideograms

•

A Chinese light
awakened me,
stolen now the dream
you were lying
in my arms
beside a little stream

•

If only
nothing
were expected
nobody'd die
waiting

•

Late fall
alone in her room
perfumed air
of evening
breeze swings
silk hangings
decorated with birds
Next morning
awakened by rain
wondering where
her lover is

•

Middle of May
strong early morning sun
breeze stirs bamboo
Cat cleaning his tail
yesterday ate
baby wren fell
from drainpipe nest,
now ignores adults'
scolding—doesn't
even remember.

•

This summer
more than before
storms miss land
Each morning
fresh flowers
in the green
peacock vase

Poem for a Painter

I have a friend
A very good friend
Who is a fine painter
Just now he paints nothing but his girl
A fat Chinese girl
With blue hair
Orange eyes
Green hands and feet
This is how he sees her
And there's no arguing it
If tomorrow she has black hair
Yellow eyes
Purple breasts
He'll have caught it right
And the wonderful thing
Is that it amuses her
Nothing more
She doesn't care that he's an artist
Or that he loves her
When her red hands disappear
Into thick blue air

Twelfth Street

for Butch Hall

Beautiful girl
hurrying home
down 12th Street
on a windy night
no way I'll ever
know her
run my hand
up her leg
while she's reading

Bar Girls

What would these girls
think of their fathers
if they could see them
moving in the gloom
and fantasy of fear
and expectation

Poem

Falling out of love
is a luxury
I never realize exists
Even now there's nothing
I can do about it
waiting on a corner
watching a woman
one leg bent
keeping her
long black hair
off her face
with her hand

Song

O fly
wouldst I
the size
of thee,
or bee,
O yes, yes
one of those,
to sleep
for ever
in a rose

To Terry Moore

for Dutch Leonard

This morning I am not
at my best
but I woke up
dreaming of Terry Moore
red apples in her sweater
sitting on a stool
in *Shack Out On 101*
sweet Terry Moore
who couldn't act
it's so painful to watch her
even in my dream
she looks uncomfortable
I want to take her in my arms
that perfect fifties body
hair shook loose over right eye
Tell me, Terry
when you were young
were your lovers ever gentle?

Claire Bloom's Face

When I was five
I fell in love
with Claire Bloom.
My mother took me
to see *Limelight*,
starring Charlie Chaplin
and Miss Bloom,
who at twenty had
the most beautiful face
I've ever seen.
We were in Miami Beach,
a cloudy day,—
I remember walking there,
the waving palms,
my mussed-up hair—

New York Movie

There you are in 1939,
blonde, bored, waiting
for the show to be over,
an usherette in a painting
by Edward Hopper on
a postcard I once sent
from New York.
I don't remember what I wrote,
I was hopelessly in love,
like Leslie Howard obsessed
by Bette Davis, everything
reminded me of you,
but what's to become of love
that's only partly true?

Phoebe's Profile

Forged on flowers
her serious
six year old's stare
What's there
inside her
pinned-up hair
eyes side-cast
as if what's past
were meant to last

A Note on Inspiration for
Duane Big Eagle

Baudelaire kept a Creole mistress
to whom he never made love
She was six feet tall
an alcoholic and a whore
Many of his *Fleurs du Mal*
were written for her
Who's to know if she ever
read any of them or cared
that he wrote her love poems
It's likely she did not
and probable that
Baudelaire died a virgin
all of which makes
for a rather sad history
Rimbaud and Verlaine, of course
fared not much better
Of those we remember
only Villon had his way
and he was hanged
The sports and divertissements
of French and other poets
are not now so easily translated
nor were they ever

Poem for Pascin

Pascin knew something about beauty
by changing his name
wearing a gold hat
We know what he dreamed
drawing girls and women
nude, in slips, unfastened dresses
his "long erotic confession"
Paquita, Hermine, Hilda, Eliane,
Léa, Claudine, Florence, Jacqueline,
Marion, Mado, Dal'Al, Zina, Mary,
Mireille, Cesarine
At forty-five, after slashing
his wrists, Pascin crawled across
the floor of his studio
and hanged himself from
a doorknob by his tie
"A man's temperament
is more important
than his work,"
Pascin said
and did his best
to prove it

Nudes

Man Ray's photograph
of three women on
the beach at Cannes
in 1933 is posed
so that only
one's face is
partly seen
Two wear hats
one stands
each is turned away
as if to avoid
exposure

Farewell Letter from Jeanne Duval to Charles Baudelaire

Charles, from the beginning you always
made me laugh. Sending flowers to my
dressing room at Le Théâtre du Pantheon
as if I were a real actress
not just the piece of fluff
trotted out for a few moments
in a brief costume
to make the boys' cocks hard.
You had money, you were charming
and respectful. You appeared impervious
to the fact of my blackness.
When we entered a café together
you were like a proud buck with his doe.
All eyes were on us as we paraded through
and you treated me as if I were a great lady;
you had the finest manners.
The apartment you bought for me
was furnished exquisitely.
It resembled a Kaliph's boudoir.
If only you had been a Kaliph!
That would have made my being a whore
more palatable. Expensive whores
live longer than the rest.
Nadar knew me before you, yes,
as did Banville.
When you first brought me to your suite
at the Hôtel Lauzun I pretended
never to have been there before.

But I had, several times, with different men,
men who knew how to satisfy a woman,
and themselves.
You created me for yourself as an object
only, a stone creature whom you could idealize
and pretend to worship and torture
yourself over. It was madness!
I'm a slut, yes, perhaps worse;
a drunkard, too. But I am *real!*
I exist *here* in this time, not in
any other and I never will.
Your reliance on women such as Luchette
and Madame Meurice has stunted you.
They encourage your impotence.
"My vampire!" you called me. It's what
you wanted, begged for, demanded.
Only by cruelty could you be convinced
of anything. Being cruel is
a soul-consuming task, and one
which amuses me to a lesser degree
than you would suppose.
I plead exhaustion, Charles.
I release myself from this obligation to you.
My sweet, poetry is not enough.

The Surrealists Come to California

Cruising in a Cadillac
down sunny 101
"Earth Angel" by The Penguins
on the radio
André Breton at the wheel
Louis Aragon and Robert Desnos,
who is dozing,
in the backseat
Breton shouts, "The old Dali
would have loved this!
The Dali of before Gala!"
"Man Ray was right about America,"
says Aragon
"All around us is
the evidence of inevitability"
"Inevitability is irrelevant,"
says Desnos, coming to life
"The true Surrealists of America
are the Oklahoma Indians
who buy big cars with oil money
and drive them until
they run out of gas,
then abandon them"
"Poor Eluard," says Breton
"he would have loved
to have accompanied us"
"Poor Péret," says Aragon
"he never kept a sou"

"Poor us," says Desnos
"snow, a woman's glove,
such gloomy symbols"
"Had Reverdy lived in California,"
says Breton
"he would never have written
'winter chased me
in the streets'"
"You must remember," says Desnos,
only one eye open
"this highway is a manifestation
of the route of Apollinaire"
"Yes," says Breton, "beauty
is no longer a nuisance"
"Or," adds Aragon, "a dream"

Delacroix's Atelier, Late October

Delacroix's painting, "Coin
du Atelier, le poêle"
from 1830, is as modern as
any work done since
Chipped bowl, smock draped
over partition, box of coal,
coat on hook, hanging vine
Shadow, grey, brown
Sudden rain shakes doves
from chestnut trees in courtyard
The museum guard sleeps in
a corner chair, still and
straight as Delacroix's stovepipe

At Apollinaire's Grave,
Père-Lachaise

A black and white cat
crawls off as I approach
Apollinaire's grave is well-kept
with many new flowers
planted in rows along
either side, two vases
filled with pink roses
in fresh water
Kostrowitzky was his name
a Pole with one strange eye
and a derby hat
A crooked stone, eight
feet high, marks his place
and Jacqueline's
Inscribed at the foot
in the shape of a heart
are the words:
Mon coeur pareil à
une flammere versée
The black and white cat
returns, looks quickly
at me and lies down
on *flammere*

At Ezra Pound's Grave, San Michele

This is the Day of the Dead
in Italy, ten years to
the day of your death
Here you are on an island
as you were in life
a paradise for mourners
Your thirst for beauty
brought you to the right place
Venice is a world beyond
you could see that clearly
Just as this is the last sun
of the year, or nearly

Redux

Walking in Kensington Gardens
with a beautiful girl after rain
I was last here fifteen years ago
Walking through this park
with another woman I haven't seen since
London doesn't seem much different
nor does the way I go
about living my life
There's something reassuring
about that, even the color
of the sky is as
I remember it, like the light
on the wall over Vermeer's
Lady Reading A Letter

Giotto's Circle

The other night
someone asked
if I ever
missed you
I thought of
Giotto's response to
the Pope's emissary
when asked
for a sample
of his work
so that the Pope
might judge
whether or not
he should be
commissioned to
paint the church
in Rome
Giotto stiffened
his elbow
against his side
and drew
on a blank piece
of paper
a perfect circle
Not wishing to
be impolite
I answered precisely
Now and again
I said
now and again

For My Winnie
at The Negresco

Missing you
for so many years
is something I
never counted on
and can't quite
figure out
When I see you
bending over or
sitting naked at
the desk in my studio
drinking Amaretto
smoking a Camel
dark blue light
blinking through
the open window
I wonder just how
difficult things
could have been
for us then that
they don't seem
any easier now

Sleepy Time Down South

You came to me last night
again in a dream
We were on a boat off
the Florida Keys
you wore a red dress,
silver earrings
your yellow hair
blew across my face
I can't imagine not
being haunted by you
If we were always together
would my dreams be half
as interesting?

Flaubert at Key West

Under waving palms
facing the grey, quiet Atlantic
over a century since
the death of Flaubert
reading again his inquiry
into the fascination
of younger men
for older women
and vice versa
This morning two butterflies
have been chasing each other
around the royal poinciana
their wings remind me of
the wide-brimmed straw hat
with a blue band
my mother used to wear
on the beach here
thirty years ago

Southern Air

The Florida sky unwraps
itself at sunset
I remember Bogart and
that bogus Bacall,
Lizbeth Scott, in
Dead Reckoning, a movie
made in Tampa in the '40s
speeding in a convertible
past palms along the Gulf
even in black and white
I could see the colors
I wish you were with me now
watching the clouds
It makes such a difference
when we're together
the sky is never enough

Tropical Street

Radio Havana still plays
1930s and '40s American tunes
Today driving on Tropical Street
I heard my grandmother Rose's
favorite song, "La Vie en Rose"
I could see her in the livingroom
of the house in Chicago
sitting at the dark brown piano
wearing a white nightgown
singing while she played
As I drove I remembered
how bright that room was
especially on a sunny morning
with snow on the ground outside
Rose died twenty-eight years ago
this month of May
so nice of her to come
and visit me this way

Blonde Light

Your scent still
on my pillow
late afternoon
of the day
after the night
we decided to
not see each
other anymore
How is it
the sun is out
or the moon
as if they've
never had enough

Traveling Light

The sound of
your voice
just now
reminded me
of an evening
wind in
the Keys
You make escape
so simple

A Chinese Note for Mary Lou

This backyard
is our Giverny—
Roses precise as Monet's,
leaning hollyhocks,
haystack compost,
sparrows on the
warped-plank bench.
Sleeping cats, black
and gray, in vine
tangle—orange, blue,
pink, red, brown,
green, yellow—all
below the Japanese sky.

Note to a Friend
Far Away

Cranes slowly
settle on
nearby pond
clouds blow through
no lovers
or friends
birds, weather
will do

Poem

A black
horse draws
lightning
I wouldn't
have thought
it possible
but today
for a moment
I could
not remember
your face

Replies to Wang Wei

(2001)

The Life of Wang Wei
by Chang Chiu-ling

I,
Chang Chiu-ling,
undertake the
task
of representing
the life
of my departed
friend
Wang Wei
he who never
failed or
forgot
me
even following
my disgrace
sent
to a far country
for the crime
of remaining
honorable
in the face
of

                    fear
              defending a
                            poor man
                who took a life
                while protecting
                          his family
My thoughts now
            are with you
                  my former companion
              borne on wings
                          of wild geese
                who fly
                            across
                  the yellow
                            river

                    •••

Native of
            Shansi
        your voice
                    and eye
          gifts from
              your mother
        despite
                  a brother
            lonely boy
          in past lives
              poet
                      and painter
          doomed to
                    reinhabit
          this universe
                    again and again

listening to
        his ancestors'
                        voices
            on the wind
    your conversations with
                secret birds
        answering until
                    the final hill
            changed
                        color
Where are
        you?

●●●

Combing snowflakes
    from
            your horse's
                        mane
    preparing
            to depart
        for the Wang River
    who could know
            which of us
            would survive
                            this
                    long separation
    I withstood
                the cold wind
                    long
                    long
            watching
                        you go
        black horse

                    stepping
                              uncertainly
              through
                        shapeless
                                  landscape

                    •••

Sounds of
          battle
       exist now
                 in
       memory or
                    imagination
       recalling the
              Kansu frontier
              your letter
                         arrived
          pages reeking
                       of woodsmoke
                  picturing
                  you
                         sitting
              in your
                    house
       in the
              Southern Mountains
          ashes
                  scattered
                       over ice
          hearing ghostly
                         hoofbeats

                    •••

Murderous dogs
    guard the imperial
        gate
  I pass silently
     head bowed
       more
            familiar now
      to his
        beasts
           than to
        the minister
   Wang
       above all
         would only
           laugh

• • •

I keep
 in
   my apricot chest
     the willow
    branch
      you gave me
    the morning
     we parted
   at Peach Blossom
        Spring
     brittle now
      I handle it
       tenderly
   How can it be
    you are
      no longer

           there
        to dangle
               your fingers
            in the bright
              green
                  water

● ● ●

Warm tears
    mark the place
    on the
          page
         where I
         had to
              stop
    Outside
              my window
        fireflies
        dot
              the air

● ● ●

I begin
    to imagine
  I understand
    the monkeys'
              noise
      as in
        your
        last days
  I am
      most often
        alone

•••

I recall your
        comment
    daylight
    disappears
        piece by
                piece
now it's
    the world
    that
    disappears
                strange
            to be so
                uninterested
            when its
                    workings
            once
                fascinated me
        now I study
                the
                falling snow

•••

Raindrops from
    heaven
        dawn
        sun
        moon
        stars
            do we
                learn
            from them

crooked

      arrows
   kill
   the swallow
   all
      perfectly
       true

• • •

So complicated
   to
be
   unhappy
you said
   and
   ultimately
      so silly
   I try
      to
   keep this
  in
     mind
  wherever that
       is

Persimmons: Poems
For Paintings

Bodhidharma

Big Dipper brow
  pours
  cinder eyes
Whiskbroom mouth
  shades chin
The winding road,
  crooked wind

  Some mind
  to wrap
the body in.

After the painting by Hakuin

Pu-tai

"Dancing" Taoist
  with bamboo
  bindle
A "wandering wise man"
  traveling
  single

  Fat and
  happy,
  head like
  a plum

No need to know
  all there is

  only some

After the painting by Liang K'ai

Monk Gazing at a Waterfall

The waterfall
fills and fills,
but there is still
the footbridge.

After the painting by Shingei (Geiami)

Two Landscapes

The way the land dips
you would almost think
there was no sea—

After the painting by Shōkei

The monk crossing
the river—
Nothing but land
on the other side

After the painting by Shinsō (Sōami)

Hui-k'o Cutting Off His Arm

Hui-k'o came to see Bodhidharma
and asked to be one of his pupils.
Bodhidharma said no, put him out
in the snow, and told him
he possessed no scruples.
Hui-k'o cut off his arm,
gave it to Bodhidharma,
and proceeded once more
with his pleading.
Bodhidharma relented, at last he consented,
and stared at Hui-k'o
who stood bleeding.
"I'm pleased you're behooved,"
said Hui-k'o, "now I've proved
my request is sincere, Bodhidharma."
"Yes," said the sage,
"your moment of rage
illumined my view
of your karma."

After the painting by Sesshū

Reading in the Study
in the Bamboo Grove

Lonely for conversation,
the scholar in the mountain hut
goes on reading.

After the painting attributed to Shūbun

Man with an Ox

The farmer's foot
on the ox's back—
The door to enlightenment
open a crack.

After the painting by an unknown artist

Kannon

Kannon's face
shows no disgrace
though he attained
no rank—
He preferred to stay
in worlds away,
where waves
break close
to the bank.

After the painting by Minchō

Persimmons

Six persimmons—
The drunkard
    stumbling down
    the hall

After the painting attributed to Mu Ch'i

Sunset in a Fishing Village

Evening haze
gathers in the shore
Fishermen taking up
their nets
Trees sink crablike
into the mountains—

one young priest
blowing kisses
to the moon

After the painting attributed to Mu Ch'i

Li Po Reciting Verse

Using *gempitsu*,
few brushstrokes
Liang K'ai captured
    a be-cloaked
    Li Po

        looking quit-caring,
        hairstrands
        tied back

        eyes sudden
        and staring

        poems in
        a sack

    The Old
    Wine Genius
wondering where's
the wine

The Sixth Patriarch
Cutting Bamboo

Hui-neng kneels
in the hills
with a razor
meditating on
Pai-chang's dictum
"A day without labor—
a day without food"
And whether
he stays or
leaves for good—
And which will
render him
less a victim

After the painting by Liang K'ai

Clear Morning
in a Mountain Village

Fogborne bands
of patchwork crows
sail liquid through
    the sun
    baring bears,
    mountain lairs
    a village
of the Southern Sung—
Below a point
two rivers join
yielding Lake Tung-ting

    One of eight
    of Yü Chien's views
    of Hsiao-hsiang

Myna Bird on a Pine Tree

Hiding his head
White-patched wing
Lone cone dangles
Trunk clawed clean
Branches descend
At irregular angles
Man never leans
The pine tree bends

After the painting attributed to Mu Ch'i

The Second Patriarch
Setting His Mind in Order

The founder of Zen
controlling his breathing—
　　Unshaven, wristleted
　　frowning in robes
Barefoot, deciding
wrinkling his nose

　　leaning on
　　an un-lean
　　cat

After the painting by Shih K'o

Landscape at Lushan

Great Waves,
High Mountains—

Home of the Dragon King

After the painting by Yü Chien

Sunrise

A monk sits mending
in the morning sun
under the poles
where the fishnets are hung
    studying thread
    drawn through
    the cloth—
One more stitch
    then
    he's off!

After the painting attributed to Mu Ch'i

Orchids and Bamboo
Beneath the Moon

Orchids, bamboo,
butterflies, snakes,
thorns in the mind,
bodiless aches.

After the painting by Bompō

Haboku Landscape

Fog surrounds the mountains.
A fishing skiff feels its way
    through shadowed water,
    avoiding the crow-webbed
    coast.

Weasels sleep in the woods.

After the painting by Sesshū

Owl on a Bare Tree

Thick black branch
In moonlight—
Owl's wise eyes

After the painting by Isshi

Sākyamuni Descending the Mountain

Exhausted by understanding
the Buddha descends,—

Enlightenment, too,
means to an end.

After the painting by Isshi

Nunobukuro

"In sleep,
gods and Buddha—
a cloth bag"

a rake rusting
in spring rain

After the painting by Hakuin

Blind Men Crossing a Bridge

Groping, hoping,
staffs a-fist,
stumbling, mumbling
cross-precipice,

Three blind men,
each right thinking—
on so narrow a bridge
there's no time
for blinking.

After the painting by Hakuin

Axe

"Chopping word"
vanquishing wickedness
with an axe.

A sharpened edge
no good man
lacks.

After the painting by Suiō

The Moment of
Enlightenment

"The clouds
are in heaven
and the water
is in the bottle"

Twisty bark
of the bo—

After the painting attributed to Chih-weng

New Moon Over
the Brushwood Gate

What peace sleeps
in the cottage
nestled in the
bamboo grove,
while the visitor
makes his bed
beneath the moon

After the painting by an unknown artist

Hotei in a Boat

Hotei in a boat
drifts amongst
the reeds
not far from shore,
meditating
on man's needs,
nothing more.

After the painting by Reigen

Rabbit and Moon

The moon
sits impaled
on the ears
of a rabbit.
Wild ducks soar
through a hole
in the purple air.

After the painting by Sengai

Landscape with Traveler
and Wood-gatherer

Without lost steps
woodsman nods
to hiker stopped
to greet him

Making good progress,
as are
the snow-shot clouds

After the painting by Aoki Shukuya

Autumn Landscape with Three Scholars Enjoying Tea by a Stream

Talking in the blowing grass,—

Words don't
bother mountains.

After the painting by Okada Hankō

Landscape with Travelers

Man and horse
man and wife
shadows still
within this life

Forest, rock,
mountain, sky

River shivers
blossoms
       fly

After the painting by Yamaguchi Sekkei

Boat on a Windy Sea

The battered seacoast cabin,
   wind-dark, creaking,
   grins in the face
   of the storm.

Water and sky slant together,
   thrashing shore
   and sailor—
   waves veer, rear
   and wail,
   make of the boat
   a wobbly pail.

After the painting by Sesson

Bell Tower at Twilight

Hiking back toward
    the temple
    a priest
    pauses
    at a stream
    to meditate.
Looking up, he sees
the bell tower ring
into darkness.

    "He who hurries
    after Zen
    is Zen,"
thinks the priest,

hurrying
to dinner.

After the painting by Ikkyū

Swallows

    swoop
swirl
      spin
  stand

flit
  twirl
  flutter

  land

Admiring swallows
the Japanese priest—

Who studies sutras?
Who suffers least?

After the painting by Ikkyū

The Fifth Patriarch
Planting Pine Trees

Hung-jen,
workingman monk
of Mt. P'o-t'ou

planted trees,
grew fuzzy hair

meditated
here & there

you could see
him hiking
bare-chested,

pine seedlings
tied to his hoe

After the painting by Takuan

Nan-ch'uan Chopping the Kitten in Two

What doesn't have meaning
never existed—
whatever took place
doesn't matter, if this did.

After the painting by Sengai

A Crow in a
Wintry Sky

How crow
can fly

       in

       grey
snow
       sky

wings white-petalled

         high

After the painting by Buson

The Road to Shu

Horses slip
up ropey path

men fall
to the rear

don't look up
don't look down

   don't

    look around

After the painting by Kindoku

Returning by Boat on
a Cold River

Along
the rocky coast

the wind
has silenced
the houses

My boat
floats
to shore

head down,
I hurry
toward home,
forsaking
the sea

Are things
any better
in the mountains?

After the painting by Chikuden

Fishermen on the Great River

So many men
depend
on the river

little wooden bridges
bound by rope

family lanterns
light the shore

the fish are bountiful

the men hope
for more

After the painting by Tessai

Crows Taking Flight
Through Spring Haze

Following fog
a flock
like a fountain

black
like the dog
with the boy
on the mountain

After the painting by Hankō

A Myriad Sounds and Thousand-layered Peaks

Gyokudō
imbiber
of sáke
& beer

Samurai,
poet,
painter
& seer

(so what
if he needed
a drink
to see
clearer?)

Building a House
in the Mountains

No ocean
no town

to know
every sound

one day
dangle my beard
on the ground

After the painting by Gyokudō

Morning Sun at Uji

Paddling past
the sleeping city

two boatmen
stare astonished
at the rising
snow-blue mountains

and do not see
the old man
on the bridge,
waving

After the painting by Mokubei

Travel Sketches
of Konodai

Fruit trees, flowers,
arriving at village

stone steps
to temple

oxcart in
road ditch

Back to
the river,
out toward
the sea

nobody notices
mountains,

or me

After the painting by Bunchō

Japan North:
Two Paintings

I.
Azechi's fisherman
black bearded, nose
                frozen
     knife, net & lures

Staring at the Ice and Snow

II.

          Saito's snowblack
                covers
                  sky

          Mother and son
          walking grey

               lamp's shadow
               warms

          Winter in Aizu

Cormorant Fisherman

Kao's cormorant
         fisherman
ragged coat
  and cap
poleing along
  shrieking
     mad
amid
  diving
white-brown
     birds

After the painting by Kao Ch'i-P'ei

Zen Poet Han Shan

Han Shan
    standing alone

I've not often seen
you this way
without your pal
      Shih-te

  Are you in a dream
remembering who
    you were
     or the face
    of a young
        girl
    some
   missing
    pearl?

*After the painting by an unknown
artist of the Late Sung Dynasty*

Han Shan and Shih-te

Laughing and pointing
away from the world
Shih-te relating
        gossip
he's heard

Han Shan's amused
    it's always
        the same
    someone to argue
    someone to blame

After the painting by Yin-t'o-lo

Lady Holding Fan

Slender lady
head inclined
hand behind
your folding
       fan

    Where was
  there ever
    your kind
      of man

After the painting by Jen Hsiung

Poems From Snail Hut

1

Back at my hut nobody bothers me
Flies buzz around my head
I lie beside yellow flowers
And watch the fog blow away.

2

Worst things that can happen:
Get bit by bugs, get poked
by pine needles or blackberry thorns
Squatting outside at night.

3

On my door I've tacked a painting
Entitled 'Door To The River'—inside's nothing much
Axe, books, broom, a container of water
Never more than three days old.

4

Fleas are my worst enemy
I give my money away
I never thought this would happen
To me.

5

I call this place 'Snail Hut' like Chao-Hsien's
Because it's so small, or 'Honeysuckle Hut'
Because of vines overhanging in the entrance
Late at night I stand dreaming in my perfumed doorway.

6

A friend once told me
To truly understand what's inside my heart
I must keep apart, remind myself
It's not necessary to be smart.

7

If often I appear righteous
It's only that
I'm still too fond
Of the world.

8

Ate, watered plants
Walked to creek
Napped in orchard
Dreaming of my children.

9

Past midnight at her loom
She is sad, sad
Such a short distance
From here.

10

When I was away
She swept my hut
Now I've returned
The dirt piles up.

11

Note to Winter Guests:
During rain snails parade
Down this path—either crush them
Or step in puddles.

12

Dreaming I'm an eagle
Gliding hills filled
With snow, watching
Horses stumbling below.

13

Sitting still, lilacs
Honeysuckle, occasional cats
Toughening mind like escaping
Past lives—highly unlikely.

14

Remembering bum outskirts of Tokyo
Ignoring ghosts, half-drunk
On an un-lit lane
Going again to sleep in the field.

15

You used to come down the stone path
To my tiny hut—it's crazy but
I still look for you there
I sit & stroke my blue-dark hair.

16

So often full of bitterness
I don't want to be
But nothing else can make me speak
It truly is the heart I seek.

17

Tonight shat in the rain
Warm breeze in my face
Last night a stray dog
Did it in the same place.

18

Late at night I lie alone
And listen to the trains blow by
Their whistles wind me down to sleep
And set the dogs to cry.

19

I'd rather be alone here than anywhere
Large apples bend the tiny tree
At night there is almost always
A soft wind.

20

Without you
Everything's
Vague as
Blue horses.

Horse hauling timber
out of Hokkaido forest

Horse hauling timber
out of Hokkaido forest

logging done in winter
to utilize snow cover
all that timber
cut by hand
curved axes, saws
& horses dropped dead
pulling sled
were left for wolves

Night Train to Mt. Yatsu

The Japanese brakesman
with his lantern
runs along the track
holding his hat,
light flickering
in the red-dark cold.
On the platform at Tachikawa,
where we wait to change
to the 2 A.M. train
to Kobuchizawa,
passengers rinse their faces
at open-air washstands,
others sit, some sleep,
in the tiny rest shack,
or walk around
trying to keep warm.
The brakesman has disappeared.
I am as lonely as ever.

Rising Sun Sonnet

Here on the mountain
the seasons shift constantly—
already this morning
it has rained, snowed,
and several branches
have broken in the wind;
now the sun is out,
but there are black clouds
to the south.
The woodcutter's wife,
back bent
by another load of sticks,
pays no attention
to the weather.

Toward Dusk

Crossing
    rickety
  fish pond
      bridge—
  Almost November,
    the woodcutter
        &
          his wife
still
    working.

Morning at Mt. Yatsu

Woodpecker woke me—
walked outside
& found a brown-furred moth
wing dots like pine knots
suspended by feelers
from spiderweb
blood sucked out
twisting in wind
on the sunny porch.

At Bikky's Workshop

for Bikky Sunazawa

Woodchips strewn
   like islands
Poets talking
   Bikky working
carving
   masks, souls—
         Ainu eyes
            in
         lost-ghost
          stolen
           faces

Poem

I am no painter
but when
a red bird
bursts from
green pine
into a grey
rain sky
it leaves itself
a part
of my
eye

Furo-ya

At the public bath
in Kokubunji
the old lady ticket-taker
eyes all the new young men
ones she knows
bore her
but it's obvious
she has her
favorites

At Nishi-kokubunji

Young Japanese girl
        flirted
            from across
                tracks
    when her train came
        boarded quickly
    sat facing the other way

North of Tokyo

Mist rising over Northern Honshu
  mountains
muddy Katsura river
with Suwa Yu on our way to Tsuru
old lady legs wrapped in brown blanket
looks out train window
silkworms crawling on kuwa plants
Suwa Yu smokes, stares at greenness
once a week he makes this trip
to teach at a country college
then it's back to Tokyo
traffic & buildings
but on the corner of his street in Nerima
you can watch the junkman
carefully cut & sort
stacks of cardboard, wire & pipe

Poem in the Style of Wang Wei

The pain in my heart does not stop
My stomach quakes
I am in love with two women
Between whom I find it impossible to choose
Glimpses of faces
What distinguishes one from the other?
They'll soon be gone
       forever from everyone
Not just an unnoticed stranger
       on the street.
Alone on a hill high above town
Nothing bothers me but what's in my head.

Buddhist Poem

On a wood bench
in Daitoku-ji courtyard
rain dripping off
enclosure roof
gong ringing irregularly.
Let go! it says
Let go! Let go!
Does it make any difference?
Is there ever a sensible decision?
What kinds of birds are there here
that never let me see them?
O this is painful
falling in love
& out & in again—
Better to shave your head,
don't take girls to bed,
devote your life to tea instead.

Poem

In Iwatsuki
an old man
pedals by
buckets strung
from shoulders
one eye shut
or out

The Last Words of Arthur Rimbaud
(2004)

Place: The Hospital of the Immaculate
Conception, Marseilles, France.

Time: November 9, 1891. The day before
Rimbaud's death.

ARTHUR RIMBAUD, *37 years old, the poet and adventurer, lies*
dying in a hospital bed. He drifts in and out of consciousness, deliri-
ous with pain. His right leg has been amputated due to a
malignancy.
    At his beside sits his sister, ISABELLE RIMBAUD, *31 years*
old. The bed is surrounded by candles, flickering in the otherwise
darkened room.

ARTHUR: Tell them, tell them ... say that I am entirely par-
alyzed, yes, and so I wish to embark early. Please let me know
at what time I should be carried on board.

ISABELLE: My poor Arthur, it's impossible for you to travel.
You can't be moved.

ARTHUR: I'll return to Harar, to Djami, he'll be waiting. I'll
return with limbs of steel, dark skin and furious eyes. With this
mask, people will think I am of a strong race.

ISABELLE: Forget Djami, forget him. I'm here, Isabelle, your sister. Think of me, of our mother, the ones who love you most.

ARTHUR: My name carved in stone at Luxor, only the wind and sand can erase it. Tell Djami I am coming, I will see him again soon. My one friend, my only friend.

ISABELLE: Djami cannot help you, Arthur. That boy is far from here, in Abyssinia. Probably dead.

ARTHUR: Send him money, three thousand francs. Tell him his master, who loves him, begs he make wise use of this sum, that he invest it prudently in an enterprise sure to realize a profit. Tell him not to be idle. His wife and child must prosper.

ISABELLE: Arthur, pray. Forget Africa.

ARTHUR: Djami and I ... two ghosts ... slipping through the subtle air. Sons of the sun.

ISABELLE: All the years away from France, broiling in the heat, your brain was affected.

ARTHUR: Capsule rifles, two thousand-forty at fifteen Marie-Therese dollars each. Sixty thousand Remington cartridges at sixty dollars the thousand. Tools of various kinds valued at five thousand-eight hundred dollars. Total value of caravan forty thousand. Fifty days to Menelek, king to pay us on arrival. We leave from Tadjoura. Ivory, musk, gold. The Choans would have our testicles! French testicles. Harar to Antotto, twenty days. Avoid Dankalis, evil savages. Sixty thousand dollars, exchange at Aden, 4.3 francs, equals 258,000 francs. Coffee or slaves. Won't take Egyptian piasters. Caravans form at Djibouti. Did I marry the Somali girl? She went back, Djami sent her away. Not my orders. Find Djami, quick! My leg, must rest my leg before meeting the Emir. Turks and cannons.

ISABELLE: [*praying*] Oh Lord, I weep! Lord, soften his agony. Help him to bear his cross. Have pity on my brother, his poor soul that writhes on earth. Have pity and take him, oh Lord. You who are so good, so kind.

ARTHUR: The hyenas laugh at us. Their laughing keeps me awake. Smelling my wound. Poetry poured from the open wound, words spilled until there was nothing left. Emptied, I fled. Djami, your warmth. She is far off, master, to BarAbir. Far, far. Cannot go there with accounts due. The business. Cheated by Menelek, cunning, cunning. *Le Bosphore Egyptien*, my case. Ragged, dirty rags, no way for a French citizen. Dead before my time, the late Arthur Rimbaud. I have been bitten by life before and survived. Two terrible years and nothing to show.

ISABELLE: Arthur, do you know me? Do you know your sister, your youngest sister, Isabelle? Can you feel my strength, my love? The love of the Lord that flows through me.

ARTHUR: I see you, my angel. My angel of happiness.

ISABELLE: Oh, yes! Yes, Arthur! I am! Your angel. Oh, thank you, Lord, for bringing my brother home before . . . before. . . .

ARTHUR: Before his death. The death of the late Arthur Rimbaud.

ISABELLE: No, perhaps it is possible that you may live! The Lord is merciful, it's in His power to heal.

ARTHUR: We'll walk then, you and I, around Harar, when my new leg is attached, my artificial limb. You won't believe the colors! And Aden, we'll journey to Aden. I can arrange things there, arms for the South. Tell Djami, my man, my one brother under the sun, I am on my way! I'm coming with snow on my scarf, flowers from the Ardennes, things he's never seen! Wake me before the harbor burns. It will burn after our boat departs, so we can watch the flames from the deck as we disappear over the horizon, a spectacle of fire, our farewell.

ISABELLE: Arthur, Arthur! Are you gone?

ARTHUR: Sails . . . yellow, red . . . the sea.

END

As If It Were a Photograph
Poems After Vermeer
(2004)

Woman in Blue
Reading a Letter

She is pregnant
I'm certain
and the letter
is from her husband
a merchant traveling
on the continent
It's possible
that he will not
be with her when
the child is born
and that the child
is not his

The Milkmaid

Holding the pitcher
her blue skirt
broad forehead
bread and milk
thick light
pours out

Woman with a Water Jug

Unlike the milkmaid
this woman is
happy
perhaps unconvinced
of the permanence
of her condition
at least she appears
confident and aware
of the importance
if not the meaning
of light

Girl Asleep at a Table

Perhaps she's
not drunk
merely fallen asleep
in an empty house
soon roused
by thunder
to stand for a moment
and watch the rain
on the rooftops
of Delft
before closing
the window
There was once
a dog in the doorway
but Vermeer painted
it out

Diana and Her Companions

Having one's feet washed
is one of life's
greatest pleasures
Diana's powerful arm
protruding breasts
early evening
in Heaven

Christ in the House
of Martha and Mary

Red and gold surround
Martha's deranged eye
Mary offering
the loaf
eyes closed
as if it were
a photograph

The Procuress

Vermeer and his friends
of the four only Vermeer
looks at the camera
as the picture is taken
he is disengaged
raising a glass
to himself
unaware of his friend's
hand on the whore's
brilliantly yellow breast

Officer with a Laughing Girl

The topographical map of Holland
made by Balthasar van Berckenrode
an open window
dashing soldier
simple girl
nothing between them
but dust in
the light

The Glass of Wine

He pours
she drinks
lute on
a chair
wood, porcelain,
silk

The Little Street

Women and children
broken red clouds
details of
immaculate quiet

Woman and Two Men

Only one pays
her attention
the other despairs
The woman
is not lovely
the man supporting
her hand is
grotesque,
capable of
murder

Woman with a
Pearl Necklace

Her self-fascination
is exceeded
in intensity
only by the extent
of our perspective
on her isolation

Woman Weighing Gold

It is because we die
that nothing lasts
There is nothing
profound in
The Last Judgment
gold, strings
of pearls are
no less limited
in value by
their replaceability

The Music Lesson

Music, companion of
joy, balm
of sorrow
the woman stands
at the keyboard
face reflected
in the mirror
white pitcher on a tray
on a table covered
with a red tapestry
the feeling is
of late afternoon
a delicate hour

The Concert

We see the beginnings
of her hands
an accompanist
audience of one
patterned tiles
keep our distance
the painting
unlistenable

Girl with a Pearl Earring

A puzzle
with blue and gold
Arab headwrapping
long earring
face of alabaster
startling
green eyes

The Art of Painting

Why are Clio's
eyes closed
History inspires
pedants
lips and eyes
measuring devices
of dreams

Lady Writing a Letter

This woman
is well to do
and unafraid
she wears the confident
air of good fortune
Her husband is
not to see this letter
Vermeer's
women disguise
their infidelities
poorly

Lady with Her Maidservant

The maid delivers
a letter from
the lady's lover
the lady's surprise
is undisguised
she could not
be dressed
more elegantly
the maid more drab
or knowing
undisguised, also,
disgust

Shooting Pool in the Dark
(2004)

Rue des Abbesses

Beauty will drive
  you mad
      it'll tear
  you up
      destroy
  people's lives—
if you
  can
  choose,
it's not
  love

Poem

It's terrible
 that I don't have
a photo of you
  I tried to draw
 pictures of you
   from memory
 but I don't like
 any of them
The truth is
  that I don't
want a drawing
   or a photo
 I want you
  I need to feel
  your hands
 on me
  and your
 tropical
   mouth

Your Face

Late autumn
and your face
is changing
When we met
the air was warm
I saw the wound
beneath your beauty
Sometimes now
when we're together
this scar disappears
and there you are
a young girl again
without pain
Last night, lying
in each other's arms
in your daughter's bed
you asked me,
What will happen
when we're *really*
in love?
I only know
I adore you more
every day
that the wind
won't blow the leaves
back onto the branches
My love, it's
late autumn
and my face
is changing, too.

Poem

That the thought
of losing you
is even in my head
disturbs me
I've never cared
for anyone
in this way before
never thought
that I could make
such a mistake
to fall in love
with the real girl
of my dreams
Now it's too late
the hunter captured
by the game
You sleep
with my soul
in your mouth
When we kiss
I can taste it

A Dream

As I told you
        last night
    we were walking
    in a dark forest
we got lost
        from each other
    I had to find you
    I called your name
you answered
            but your voice
        was faint
    as if you were suddenly
    impossibly far away
        I followed the sound
for what seemed
            like days
        I didn't want
        to give up
        to leave you alone
        in the forest
I didn't know if
    you were really lost
            or where I was
        Finally, I saw you

walking along a path
I didn't know was there
You stopped by a tree
I waited to see
which way you would go
I heard a noise
behind me
and looked around
but nothing moved
Now you were
beside me
and we moved together
along the path
You took my hand
It's true, you said,
I'm a little lost
I followed you anyway
The path disappeared
but we kept going
This is love, I said
You turned and kissed me
Yes, you said, I know.

My Last Sonnet

I don't know if you remember me,
I'm the boy you danced with
at the Communist picnic in Albarese
We were so in love the bad music
didn't matter, or the weather, clothes glued
to our bodies by sweat as we swirled
Your brothers, their wives and children
seemed amazed by us, the way we danced,
how happy we were—
What happened, my love?
How did we fall?
I feel like Icarus, wings gone
sinking in the sea under the terrible weight
of his father's heart

Brigands

Your dream of Sardinia—
    you were there once
    at fifteen
Your older brother
    taught in a village,
married a Sardinian girl
    You ran by the sea,
    listened to tales of bandits—
    briganti—
hiding in the mountains,
    only women in the villages—
The *briganti* sneak down
        at night
    to visit—
your fantasy to be stolen
    away, held
captive, ravished, used
    by rough men,
    one day taught to
    fire a gun—
rifle over your shoulder,
        barefoot
    brigand girl—
You should have gone back
    alone, years ago
    when Sardinia
    and you
    were still wild

Life & Death with an Actress

Your idea
    of love
is
    Duel in the Sun
    your ideal
    woman
    Kleist's Penthesilea
    who killed
            Achilles
        then ate
        him
Spared now the burden
        of having to die
        to prove
                my love
    I hereby abdicate
        this role
    in which I was
                involuntarily
    if not unwittingly
                cast
        Take pity
        if you can
            on
        my replacement
        may he
            be agile
        as Achilles
    but fearful

Letter from La Habana

Imagine lying in bed
three in the morning
with a pretty mulatta,
she sings for me
a romantic tune
from her not distant childhood
as waves slither
along the beach
accompanying a little wind—
I think of
savage Penthesilea
in Kleist's story, crazed
by unexpected desire
to destroy her chance
at happiness, misunderstanding
Achilles' submission,
devouring him
with her dogs, doomed
thereafter, a ghost of love—
I understand you now,
my Cuban girl's song
lost to myth, the elegant night
caught in her impossible throat.

Unsent Letter from La Habana

In the Cuban night
color of Havana Club
I stared at the black sea
raising itself above the Malecón
an ancient, stubborn beast
trying again and again
to climb ashore
to get back to where
once he had been
And I thought of you
dancing in that beautiful room
high above the white streets
of San Francisco
while I played the piano
looking out a window at clouds
color of sand at Varadero
How to get back, I thought
what miserable beasts we are
how impossibly stubborn
to be in love forever

Boca Chica

It was all a long time ago
    walking next to you
        beside you
            dropping behind
                        a little
                to watch your ass
                    as if one fist were
                    being placed over the other
            stepping like a cat
                    your mother said
                    Arabs stopped to look
            Were we on the Boulevard Magenta?

                            I wanted it
                            right there
                in front of everyone
                            or no one
        I got it later
        only it was so
                    long ago
            I don't remember

Shooting Pool in the Dark

Living with you
is like shooting pool
in the dark
impossible to guess correctly
which ball to hit next
or even know what stripe
or solid, number or color
is still there or where
Life with you is like
being asked to run
a neverending table
blindfolded and bleeding
from a shotgun wound
I once saw Willie Mosconi
run 91 balls in a row
shooting straight pool
at Benzinger's in Chicago
I'd bet anything
he couldn't have done it
with a hole
this size
in his heart

True Love

Your sickness made me
a little sick, it's
true—I still
feel it
  Mayakovsky got down
    on his knees
and declared
        his love
to his last
        mistress
    a few hours after
      he'd met her
Remember me
at the hotel
        in Paris,
  on my knees
    in the lift?
We're all the same
men of too much passion
and a little talent—
  some a little more
        than others
We fool ourselves
  into thinking
      we're strong
    then complain
    the rest of our lives
    crippled by
      the consequences

Memento

I miss seeing the magnolia
tree
in the courtyard
out the kitchen window
every morning
I remember how upset
you were
after its limbs
were trimmed
I was away when it happened
you were afraid
I'd be unhappy
to see it
but seeing you
was all that mattered
The magnolia
did look sad
nude and frightened
shivering even in
the Roman sun
and you
trembling in my arms
a perfect
fallen
blossom

Back in America
(2004)

Back in America

Old cowboy
  crossing Oakland
       street
    with rodeo limp,
  spotted face
     and hands
  boots scuffed, cracked
    filthy shirt
      untucked—
  stuffed in left
    back pocket
  of faded jeans
  The Iliad—
if only Homer
  could see him,
  headed
    to dump hotel
    half-pint
    of bad bourbon
     in bag
      dreaming glories
     of Greece
    and his
      lost
    horse

On Viewing the Manuscript Scroll of Jack Kerouac's Novel On the Road in the Tosca Bar, San Francisco

Lying in state, under glass,
partially unrolled to reveal
flood of words describ'd
Mississippi River near New Orleans
1947—an American Shroud,
Davia Nelson called it, like
the Shroud of Turin, holy remnant
of modern literature, naively
woven tapestry—
        Kerouac would have lov'd
this I think, his own worn
Shrouded Stranger, well-travel'd
displayed for religious purpose,
himself collapsed Catholic Buddhist
pilgrim in constant search
for the Sacred, sanctified today
here in sere mute Tosca cathedral
light, lone silver'd stream of sun,
God's finger pointed toward window
sarcophagus casket containing
phantom tome brought out by hand
half-century before by Jack Kerouac
from America's burning Egyptian heart.

                    10 May 2001

Small Elegy for Corso

to Fernanda Pivano

Gregory Corso's buried in Rome
a few weeks ago next to Shelley
in an *acattòlico* cemetery in Testaccio
Sitting on a bench in the Piazza Cavour
I recall Nanda telling me last December
Gregory had his balls cut off
"I don't care," he told her, "I fucked enough."
Now at twilight in the Quartiere Prati
watching rich women walk big dogs
past palm trees under plum-colored sky
suddenly there's Corso ten years ago or more
at a baseball game in San Francisco
shouting at a player, "Pull up your pants!
It's a disgrace to the uniform!"
Three rows in front I looked around,
"Gregory," I said, "what happened to
your teeth?" "They're gone!" he said
"Who needs teeth after fifty?"
We met again at a wedding in Bolinas
Quietly he told me how secretly he
envied Kerouac having died so young,
only 47. "If only he could have enjoyed
himself more, but he was always drunk."
O Gregory, may you take eternity for all
it's worth, the same as you captured
your time on earth, knowing all along
there was nothing real to lose.
Roll over, Captain Poetry,
tell old Percy the news.

25 May 2001

In Memory of Suwa Yu

Creek
        crawling through
                woods
How many thousands
                of years
                without stopping
        I'm happy
        to listen
                longer
        than that

The Day Allen Ginsberg Died

I got up early
looked out the window
at a freight passing
on the Hudson
sun poking out
reluctantly, a colder day
than expected
I'd heard the night before
Allen was sick and dying
given only a few
months to live
Odd to find myself
in New York, his city
at the moment
of his passing
the newspaper said
he had recently completed
a new book entitled
Death and Fame
This afternoon I visited
one of my oldest
and best friends
who a few days before
had told me his father
was not expected to live
more than a few weeks
His father was
a tough guy
I'd always liked him
a working class guy

from Chicago
where he still lived
His son called him
while I was there
and handed me the phone
The old man sounded
as strong as he always
had—difficult for me
to believe he'd soon
be gone
He called me by a
childhood name
and suddenly
I teared up
No way to stop this
I thought.
Now Allen G. dead
gone to greet
Jack and Neal
after almost thirty years
I imagine Jack
in Buddha Heaven
saying, Thanks for
coming, Al
This morning is his funeral
I decide not to go
figuring it will be
a mob scene
I don't like funerals
anyway and what's
the point
At nine a.m.
When the Buddhist ceremony

is scheduled to begin
a four hour affair
culminating in cremation
the doorbell rings
I have a vision of Allen
standing at the door
saying, I didn't die
but I don't want to miss
this. Come with me!
But instead it's
the plumber
I first met Allen
thirty-one years ago
in London
He'd come with his
father Louis to give
a poetry reading
A few years later
we worked together
editing a book
of his and Neal's letters
I last saw him
two years ago
in Paris
We met on the
rue de Sèvres
he showed me a medal
the French minister
of culture
had awarded him
He told me
how good I looked
kissed me wetly

on both cheeks
Allen wrote
Death stay thy phantoms!
and was allotted his
three score and ten
He and Kerouac
were two of
my greatest inspirations
when I was a kid
They gave me hope
that beauty and meaning
could be found
amid the chaos
I told him
this once
and Allen said
Keep hoping!
Hiking together
on a trail
at Gary Snyder's
Kitkitdizze in 1976
we came upon
a pile of ashes
and stepped carefully
around them
Allen's ashes
are to be buried
by Louis's grave
In death we return
to the father
Farewell Allen
you're with
the phantoms now.

Bordertown

Bordertown

        is a place to make money,
                spectacles to
           attract tourists,
     a sopa picante with
                  a touch
                     of evil

      ****

       Man knifed on Juarez
          sidestreet,
             stiff after
       two days,
          his stink
    not even noticeable
or defined among the
     general stench
  by Club Colorada
A miniature Yolanda all
       mouth and eyes
   shimmering in
       a doorway

****

Bordertown is the city of spooks,
       of greedy ghosts

and unapproachable
visions

****

Dirt streets of
deep southwest
pariah dogs groan
in the fabulous dust
and heat,
flies laying eggs
on chickens
and hanging
pigs

******

The only certainty is
at the cemeteries, the
only grip
on life to visit and
revisit
the acknowledged dead
The living dead pay homage
to each other's fate,
a place to
finally meet
and be restful

Impossible to be at
peace
in this crush,

this pesthole
life built
on the refuse of
El Norte

*****

Whores in the broken
light like
giant parrots,
birds ready
to peck your eyes
and pick your pockets
At the same time
become dreamy
Aztec princesses muy sincero
y las románticas
de sus sueños

*****

The ramshackle countryside
devours the border sun,
thin wind
tickles scabrous brush
as border patrol run down
rats scurrying
from the rotten
stinking sinking
ship
like piñatas falling
off the back

                    of a speeding
                      truck

        *****

Here's where the road
      ends,
             in the ground or at water's edge—
             Boca Chica, the girl's
                   mouth,
                          the gates
                                 of hell
          or heaven
                 swung
                 wide,
                      waiting to
                           receive you,

      the same in death
           as in life,
                    forever.

Rainy Tijuana

Riding slow in taxi
    rainy night Tijuana
      tiny whore
    red skirt
        tilting
      on spike heels
        darts pink tongue
            through
          silver paint lips
        her bare
      bird shoulders
        make me shiver

Monk in the Morning

for Al Young

I love to listen to Monk
in the morning
Those tilted notes
hit me
just right
It's the way I feel
before the world
gets into
my head
pulls me
kicking and screaming
out of those
brilliant corners
"Coming on the Hudson"
is my speed
slow blue steps
up toward
as much consciousness
as I can handle
Monk's music is stolen
from dreams
anyway
Only Thelonious
could get through that
door
the only one
with the right
key

American Music

Dusk, Oakland—
girl in window
leaning on a pillow, smoking
she resembles
Billie Holiday
four flights up
pudgy, bored
exhaling desire
into the already fetid
late summer air

Shanghai Garden

I'd be confined
              to dreams
      were it
              not
      for the
              blue dragonfly
        just landed
              on
                  my hand

Chinatown Carnival Night

Wizened Chinese bum
slumped on bench
grimy sack by sandaled feet
toes torn and black
Portsmouth Square San Francisco
bloodflecked beard
oozing eyes
surrounded by people
passing unseen
lost from their world
suffering this last indignity
going soon to drink
endless cups of rice wine
in the better company
of heavenly dragons

Change in the Weather

For years I was lost
in the eye of a hurricane
rain and wind enshrouded my heart
I couldn't see beyond the clouds
Now the sky's brightness
almost blinds me
but sometimes I catch you
hiding behind your eyes
the most beautiful eyes
I've ever seen
I kiss them tenderly
hoping you'll allow me
to see you as nobody else
not even you
ever has

September 11, 2001

The Chinese
        used
            to say
    in parting
from a person
                perceived
        as an
                adversary
    "May you live
        in interesting
                times."
    This is
        our new
        address

Late September in Toronto and the Weather is Still Fair

I love these
      young girls
         proud
   of
      their breasts
As we pass
      on the street
      they confess
         everything,
      knowing how
            easy it is
            for me
         to forgive
               them

Adios, Chico!

Kid Gavilian is dead
in Miami, a Cubano welter
who couldn't beat Sugar Ray,
not in New York, anyway—
He had a bolo
but no real punch, and
a face like a frying pan
full of sizzling
chicken livers

Eurydice in Romania

Gorgeous Gypsy girl, perhaps
fifteen or sixteen,
wrapped in a silver and black
striped strapless dress,
wearing high heels, big sunglasses,
waist-length cobalt hair
brushed by the breeze, strolling
next to the narrow, crumbling highway—
Is she a prostitute? I think not,
just a kid done up on
a boring Sunday afternoon—
she could be on a runway in Milan,
strutting for Valentino,
instead of parading in the drizzle
on a lonely road
through the Carpathian mountains—
I look back, but
she's disappeared
and I hate that I'll never
see her again.

near Vatra Dornei
1 June '03

*Las cuatro reinas/*The Four Queens

(2006)

Who holds
the
four queens
knows what
it means
when the air
turns
black
inside your
brain
and
the room
screams
Estrellita!
written in
spilled whiskey
on the
table
before your
head
hits it
hard

There she is
letting
you want
it
she's a saint
don't cross her
or you
wake up
with
the devil
sitting on
your
chest

Teresa this is the last
beer I swear
                or if
   not for sure
            tomorrow
   yeah I be home
                    then don't
                  hate me

All of us
on the
outside
            are
dead

What the church
is for
is
to
forget

Oh baby
　　you got a
good chance
　　　　with me
　　you know?

It's sooner
than
    you think
    you think

A room
can always
become
smaller

Hey Pete
    take a look
  at what
He done
      with the
  sky
    today

Ain't gettin'
out
anytime
real
soon

When *Estrellita*
she sang
it was
always
so
beautiful

You can
 no
  give me
 more trouble
  than I have
   already have

Rodolfo Fierro
El Carnicero
once shot a stranger
in Ciudad Chihuahua
to settle a bet
as to
whether a dying man
would fall
forward
or backward
Fierro predicted the
man
would
fall forward
he won
the bet

I like you
baby you
got
to taste
it

That road broke
my heart
too much
times
already
man
you goin'
without
me

Her name
was Julieta
she had tiny
perfect
ankles
thin
as knitting
needles

I ask her
  if the damn
 thing ever
     come in her
  she said
      Every time

What you doing
that for?
Can you do
something for
me *Chico*
come on

Why you want to
worry what it ain't
seguro
ain't
no way
to
forget

It got broke
in Guerrero
mi *esposo*
Felipe
put
a nail
in his eye

Remember when
        the wolf
    stole that
        baby
    raised it up
was a good
        wolf

Her eyes were like
black lakes
could drown in
there
carnal
believe
it

Don't look like
nothin' now
boy
you come
back
2 a.m.
bring
your *pistola*

Now there's a man
know how to do
some serious damage
to a woman
whether she got
black stripes
down her back
or not

Chinese flew to Mexico
disguised as birds
changed back to
human form
when they landed
on the ground
that's how come
there's Chinese
everywhere

We preserve
    ourselves among
ignorant beasts
        by appearing
    as angels

The chicken his name
was Octavio
    he would
    follow me around
    Octavio ate corn
    from the palm
    of my hand
    he never pecked me
    with his beak
      my cousin Rodrigo
      murdered him
      with a hatchet
        put Octavio's head
        on my pillow
          I was seven
            years old
          I still have
          that pillow
          with Octavio's blood
            on it

I kill
that
fuckin' dog
take a brick
to his
bony
head

In Mexico some people
believe birds work
for the devil
they fly around
and identify
for Satan the weak
and wicked
whom he comes for later
to my knowledge
there are no birds
in hell

Callejon de los Manzanares
narrow canvas covered
bare
lightbulb lit
alleyway
lost backstreet
Tepito central district
Mexico City slum market
Cantina La Grande
putas on parade
circle
like paddock racehorses
as men with dangerous mouths
navaja switchblades
in pockets
tilt against walls
looking to choose or just
to look—
Women and girls all sizes shapes
ages
though none more
than forty
my guess—
a few giggling
joking as they
quickly walk
others somber pachydermic
stare straight ahead—
little kids run in and out
like playground
their grandmothers
Aztec stonefaced in wallhole

                              blanket doorways—
        hawknosed darteyed
                              icepick *pistolero*
                    nightowl muggers slouch in bars
                    alongside
        while *Chilango tango* growls
                              bewailing this
                    impossible sad savage
        somehow poignant
                              tender ritual
    Catholic Indian sideshow
                    of Evil
        fate born out
                              ancient
                    bloodthirsty sins

Hidalgo goes every day
to sit and wait
    it's where his son Diego
        was last seen alive
            Even though
                    the boy's
            bones were found
                in an abandoned house
                    in Mexico City
                two years ago
            Hidalgo still sits
                and waits
                    he told his wife
                        Elena
                    that Diego's spirit
                        sometimes comes
                        to the spot
                        to visit
                The color of Diego's
                                spirit
                        is metallic
                        blue

What if a big
ball of fire
fell on the earth
from space
and it rolled
across the planet
burning up everything
and nothing could
stop it
even rich people
would die

I used to have
a bicycle
like that
Good for you
now
I have it

Paloma gave it
up to me in
the balcony
man they can't
tear down
my memory

My father rode with
Pancho Villa when
Villa attacked Columbus
New Mexico
the only time
the United States
was ever invaded
on their land
Children here don't
know who Villa
was
they only want
to go to Disneyland

Bad weather
never bothers me
it's a reminder
that no human being
has control over
anything
that's why I try
never to tell
anyone what
to do or
say
Cars and trucks
either they run
or
they don't

I don't go anywhere
        ever
            This isn't much
            of a life
            I'm glad it's
        not the only
                    one
            I've
                    got

My mother's name
was Rosa
she made *tortillas*
she died last year
she couldn't hold a
                    cup
    in her fingers
because of the arthritis
    My father left
        my mother and
            three children
    when I was six
        she told me
        he was shot
    and died in Matamoros
        a couple of years
                        later
I got this
    girl and
a boy
        no man
        now
    but we doing fine

I got almost
all the way now
through my life
and I never hated
another person
no matter what
anyone done
How many people
you know
could say this
without it
be a lie?

Don't eat
   my children
  take me
      I taste
  sweet
   in your
      mouth

Do it again
           that way
      from behind
                I don't
      care
           out here
           nobody can
     hear
        me scream

Kick it again
maricón
I tell
every
body

If you don't
know who
you are
I ain'
goin' to
tell you

Somewhere up
there
they found
her
body
man
I heard
it
was pretty
fucked
up

Nobody told me
just a feeling
let's not
stay
here
Okay honey
keep the
beads

I did for
her
was all for
her
she gone to
Big D
with José

Happen right here
four thirty
in the morning
you never seen
so
much blood

How could I know
he have
    a shotgun
was up
  in my face
  so
    fas'!

Why there gotta be
so much
ugly things
down here
better you
just
look up

Man don'
             tell me
      that no
             real
         woman
      anyway
         I take
             her

That old DelRay
he come stormin' out
wavin' that
switchblade
Buddy coldcocked
him with a tire iron
that's his head
lyin'
over in the bush
red ants
ate out
the eyeballs

Paco tell you
do something
you
do it
what you
Paco's
puta now

In the end
it all
comes down to this
don't it
It's a losin' game
I know
but it's
the only
one
counts

I remembered Veracruz
even though I'd never
been there
  These are the very
best kinds
of memories
    those
immune from fault
or doubt
that cannot be
    corrected
I will live in
the stars
    above
Veracruz

Imagining Paradise

New Poems

The Poet at the Hôtel Sordide

Baudelaire died from
                syphilis
        although his friend
        Nadar
                        insisted the poet
                remained a virgin
        throughout his lifetime
                Toward the end
                        he was destitute
                        practically catatonic
                decaying
                                in a dingy
                                        nursing home
                Madame des Molènes
                                visited him
        saw to it
                        that for the first time
                        in weeks
                        he was bathed
                                and groomed
                She held up a mirror
                                to his face

Having not seen
         his reflection
     for almost
              a year
     moved by the sight
       of this white-haired
           bearded
                 frail figure
     Baudelaire bowed
            as one would
       to any
            new acquaintance

Monk's Funeral

Snowy February day in New York 1982
    I read in newspaper Thelonious Monk's funeral
open to public I trudged crosstown
        through drifts to get there
    Saint Peter's church Lexington & 54th
woman handed me program at the door
      went in sat down on bleacher seat
3/4 round auditorium with windows so people
outside pressed against glass looked in
    sat behind Sandman Sims famous tapdancer
also Amiri Baraka and Monk's family
    with them the Baroness Nica de Koenigswarter
in whose apartment Charlie Parker died 1955
he was 35 the medical examiner said Bird had
    body of a man thirty years older
There was Monk in open coffin front and center
still on the bandstand dressed in a good suit
    Telegrams from Miles and Dizzy read to crowd
more than a dozen musicians played their favorite
Monk tunes: Walter Bishop, Jr., Tommy Flanagan,
Barry Harris, Charlie Rouse, Gerry Mulligan

made everyone cry with Ruby, My Dear solo
Randy Weston towering over everyone at the piano
made Monk come alive all over again
I looked at the center window a postman bag over
his shoulder nose against glass wideeyed
with frozen tears
We filed past the coffin and bid adieu
then out into the crepuscule as Monk
called his song for wife Nellie
snowflakes swirling in dim Central Park light
I walked listening Thelonious
abiding with me

The Generalissimo Waves

for Daniel Schmid

Listening to Noche de Biarritz
  watching fog lift
          here in
    San Francisco
  You once said Why don't
you live in Europe
    closer to me
  but later
    when I lived
        in Rome
   you never came
     to see me
  I think of you
    dying now
     at that hotel
     in the Alps
  I watched lightning
    heard thunder standing
     on the balcony
of my room in the Villa Selva
  snowstrewn mountains
          under the moon
    thirteen years ago
    Tabou is playing now
   the Lecuona Cuban Boys
   from the 1930s
  your favorite decade

whispery melodies
rumbas with
clever lyrics
What are you listening to? the last
sounds you'll ever hear
You won't lie still
like Proust expecting
a wildhaired crone
in a dark cape
to enter the room
you'll die reaching
for a book
a record
Bajo de Luna
on your
crocodile skin
phonograph

Looking for Nanao

In 1975, I went to Japan
for the first time.
Gary Snyder gave me a list
of people to look up,
one of whom was Nanao Sakaki.
Nanao had been a fighter pilot
during World War II.
After the war, he became
a wandering poet and
mountain climber, walking
the length and breadth
of Japan, preferring to not
have a permanent home.
"Life is impermanent," Nanao
told me. "Better to live in
the world than a house."
For more than two months
I traveled around the country,
from Honshu to Hokkaido,
finding several of Snyder's friends
but not Nanao. He seemed
always to have just left
the place in which I had
just arrived. A few days
before I was to leave Japan,
I found Nanao in Tokyo.
"I've been looking all over
for you," I told him.
"Finally you come to

the right place," he said.
The next morning, we left
the city to climb Mt. Fuji.
To get part of the way up,
we hitchhiked a ride
on the back of a truck
hauling fish. "Like fish,"
said Nanao, "we began
in water. Out of it, both
men and fish smell bad."
Before descending Fujiyama,
Nanao said, "Good you could
make it. Next time you come,
mountain might not be here."
Three years later, I met
Nanao again, this time
in San Francisco. "Is Fuji
still there?" I asked him.
"I'm not sure," he said. "I've been
away long time now. I'll go
back sometime to see."
The last I heard from Nanao
was a postcard from Papua
New Guinea, on which he'd written
two words: "Still looking."

17.IX.05

The Thief's World

I only saw the Colosseum
from the outside
I never went to the Vatican
I did see the Big Typewriter
Mussolini's wedding cake
and the piazza in Milano
where he was hanged
by his heels
The road to and from Fiumicino
over and over
Césarina my favorite restaurant
Fight and Fitness the boxing gym
The Villa Ada
under the pines of Rome
where we walked from the stables
Prati in the rain
We raced everywhere
always late
But sitting in the garden
with old Camillo
was best
he smoked
we drank beer
he showed me where he'd planted
the strawberries

Übermensch

Friedrich Nietzsche used to walk
through the woods near his house
in Sils-Maria, Switzerland, a wild-haired
old fud talking to himself, followed
by local kids who threw rocks at him.
Now kids around there go into the woods
and choose one among them to be "Nietzsche"
and chase him and throw rocks.
My friend Daniel Schmid's mother was
from Sils and he told me he used to play
this game when he visited there as
a child. We didn't know who Nietzsche was,
he said, only that there was a legend
about a crazy man who hated everyone
and roamed the forest shouting and
mumbling. The first time I went to Sils
with Daniel we sat next to a lake by
the woods eating sandwiches. I was curious
to know if Nietzsche ever chased after
the kids who tormented him or if he
tried to ignore them even when he
got beaned.

The Visit

I had a visitation last night
in a dream—my dear friend
Daniel dead eleven months
arrived in a car with two men
one his partner Thomas
the other I didn't know
They sat on the street by my house
in the car—I went out to
greet Daniel but he was reluctant
to talk to me—it was clear
the others didn't want him to—
this was due to a misunderstanding
concocted out of jealousy by
one of them as Daniel lay
on his death bed—
Thomas and the third man urged
Daniel to remain in the car
they were in a hurry to get somewhere—
We did speak but almost like strangers
I could tell he wanted us to be
as before when we called each other
brother—a decade of love laughter
and arguments a true friendship—
Suddenly they drove away
leaving me standing on the street
too much left unsaid and unresolved
though I'd tried—
I woke up and as I remembered the dream
with eyes closed I saw a letter

addressed to me in Daniel's distinctive
uneven hand written in the margin of a page
in black ink with a sharp point as
with a quill pen—I couldn't read the words—
Were they in German? (Daniel was Swiss)—
As I struggled to decipher them they
disappeared bit by bit until it
became impossible for me to recognize
anything other than his signature—
Daniel—at the bottom of the page
I must have still been half asleep
because I told my friend Vinnie
(who knew Daniel) what had happened
and he said Forget it Daniel's dead anyway—
I opened my eyes—I could still see Daniel
sitting in the car looking at me
wanting to talk—What had he written?
What did he have to tell me? Will he
ever come back?

Cocteau's Hands

So
        slender,
    long as a young
            girl's
                fingers
                curled
    Cocteau
        feigning sleep
            photo 1926
                life mask
                cradled
                        shoulder
            like Cocteau
                everything fake
            except pianist's hands
                wasted on
                a poet

Poem

What is
    a
      woman
but
   a ghost
   of desire
lost
   always—
now
   an angel's
   caress
   yesterday
     she
murdered your
      mother
   it's
    the same—
And to all
      men
   let me
    just
  say
   talking about
    women
      you
  don't
   know what
   you're talking
    about

Hey, Ludwig, Grab Yourself a Pigfoot

Monk's "Functional" (1956)
    kicks me in the same place
        as Beethoven's 3rd movement
("Adagio ma non troppo—Fuga.
            Allegro, ma non troppo")
    of his "Sonata No. 31 in A flat major,
                Opus 110")
    Monk made Beethoven over
        strolling on 63rd Street
            just whistling
        on the way home
            from the liquor store—
        or is that
                too simple?

Poem (1978)

At the sorrow bar
people leave or stay
or plead for impossible
promises—
Is anyone worth any
of it
Are the people saying
anything new
They come they go
said the poet
and they talk not only
of angels
They are at a loss
to begin with—

Faded Love

I am surrounded by death
it happens to everyone
all the time
Some people try not to notice
not me I've always known this
and paid attention
Nobody forces me to go on
I know what this means
one day I won't pay attention
and nobody will notice

The Young Girl's Crime

Come into this dream
with me, I said
Don't you wish you could?
for years from now
and I'm beyond dead
that strange it will seem
you didn't know how
or even if you would

Going to Meet Mike

Just off train
  in Philadelphia
  walking on Walnut Street
          kid loading
          cart on truck
          tattoo left biceps
  "An act of kindness
    is no sign of weakness"
        I pass
    The Lodge of
            Theosophists—

Sitting on the Porch Swing Imagining Paradise I Am Embraced By My Old Sweetheart, Emily Dickinson, Who, Among Other Things, Informs Me That She Has Missed Me Greatly

for Nick & Stephanie

Hello, Bees,
Swift and buzzing—
Tell me, please,
What you're discussing—
And Flies—you, too—
What's all this
Fussing? Why is it
You are always
Rushing? Why not behave
More like clouds,
Cruise quietly the sky—
Now—is all—we'll ever have
Until the time we die—

Remember, It's Only a Movie

Seeing again
your
face
after two or
three years
was not strange
or terrible
it didn't make me
feel sad
or nostalgic
but clinical
as if I were viewing
a creature
with whom
I had once been involved
in a terrifying
medical experiment
and now
here she was
this damaged animal
slightly altered
but still breathing
fire
and I was thankful
you were only
up there
on the screen
tearing the scenery
to shreds
instead
of me

Tuscany

We were in the Antinori castle,
guests of the man who had overseen
the vineyards for many years.
It was a Sunday afternoon, very hot,
several other people were there.
After touring the vineyards
and part of the castle, our group
were seated at a long table
sampling wines and conversing.
I got up after a short while
and wandered by myself through
the rooms until I came into one
with a portrait of a beautiful woman
on a wall and a divan covered
with red silk. I lay down on the divan
and fell asleep—the heat, the wine—
and when I awoke you were there,
sitting on the edge of the divan
looking at me. At first, I thought
I was dreaming, that it was the woman
from the painting by my side.
Then I recognized you, your face
even lovelier than hers.
You touched my lips and, very tenderly,
you kissed me. We have to go, you said.
I glanced around the room, at dust
swirling in an arrow of late sunlight,
once more at the portrait, then at you.
How cruel to not still be there,
crueller still to remember.

Al Young's Blues

Come on, Al, you
remember *The Sweet Flypaper*
of Life, Langston Hughes' text
for Roy DeCarava's photos—
Have things changed?
Let me tell you,
following a girl up a staircase,
eyes on the prize,
is still gonna get a sonofabuck
in a whole lotta trouble—
and who is there, really,
to thank for that?

After Listening to Bartók's From the Diary of a Fly

Climbing all those
  tiny steps
    to get
      to heaven
  only to be
      turned away
  without an
      explanation

View of Rain in the Tropics

It's pouring now
in Cartagena
de Indias
as it always does
in October,
huge storms
that paralyze
the city—
From the deck
of a passing ship
it's possible to see
this deluge,
to imagine
a girl, one
you knew,
on Calle de la Factoría,
her scant dress
soaked through,
forced
to take shelter
in a bar,

perhaps the same one
in which you met her,
tossing water from her
long, tangled
black hair
as she curses
and laughs,
then accepts
a drink
from the first
man
who offers

The Tiger

Last night there was
a tiger in my dream
a big, beautiful thing
moon orange, stripes
                    straight-razor
            black
                threatening
                    my family and friends—
        growling hungrily, I guessed
                he came for me
                I stood
                        still
        more amazed
                    than frightened
                Blake's cat
            the man-eater of Kumaon
                    Where was Sabu?
            but he turned away
            back into the jungle
            everyone was
                    relieved
                except me
                I missed him
                        terribly

Devil or Angel

Listening to the Clovers sing
while reading the *Canti* of Giacomo Leopardi
I can't help but consider Leopardi's lyrics
along with those of Charles Calhoun or
Lieber and Stoller and Ahmet Ertegun—
"Let the voracious bird flap his black wings
above me, let the beast have at me" whines
the Italian, while the Clovers croon
"Your cash ain't nothing but trash, but
I'm sure gonna get me some more"—
Leopardi's dogged, gloomy confessions
can't cut it next to "I told her that
I was a flop with chicks, I been this way
since 1956"—Leopardi would have had
a much better time of it had he altered
his "Love, love, long ago you flew out
of my heart, which once had been so warm,
burning even. Sorrow held it in her cold hand,
and it turned to ice" to "Love you flew clean
out of my heart, while I was hopin' we'd
never part. I was burnin' on the fly, but
you were turnin' to another guy"—
Poor Giacomo, whose "futile effort to protect
himself…from the evil game" gave him
the heebie jeebies. If only he could have
tuned in to the Clovers' warning: "Fool,
fool, fool, that I was to fall for you"—
Even a melancholic hunchback poet like
Leopardi might have lived and loved longer,
not to say written some snappier lines
to a better beat.

April Again

In Madrid
it's raining
an old man
plays "Under Paris Skies"
on an accordion
water runs down
his face
I'm on the corner
of Álcala and Gran Vía
the accordionist
kneels on a blanket
I don't care if
I ever go back to Paris
love vanishes there
I give him
two euros
anyway

A Thank You Note to Chekhov

I remember the exact moment
the fog lifted
and I realized
you really were crazy
and there was nothing
I could do about it
I was not a doctor
and you were not
the doctor's wife
When we met a year
and a half later
we behaved much as
we had before
but both of us
were calmer
and friendlier
Before we parted
you said
For the first time
I believe
you understand me
It was still
all about you
but it was enough
for me

Afteft Selim

From a Gamalia alley
I watched a blind man
trying to cross the road
amidst constant Cairo traffic
where drivers never stop
He banged his cane
against cars and trucks
as he bumped forward
Nobody helped him
Somehow he made it
his sooty white galabiyya
trailing behind
Safe on the opposite side
he leaned back his head
eyeballs rolled heavenward
Allah willed it
This is how I feel
when you and I don't connect
like that blind Cairene
staggering against the odds
When finally we find our way

back to each other
it's as if an unseen force
has intervened
probably not Allah
but who knows
All I know is
the traffic doesn't stop me
from trying to get to you
despite my blindness
I keep hoping you're there
waiting for me
on the other side
of this impossible street

Genealogy

In the Egyptian
Museum
in Cairo,
there is a manuscript
room—
I went back to
it twice
to study
the wend
and warp
of
ancient hands,
knowing
my own
guided
by theirs

The Poet's House

In Alexandria, in Cavafy's apartment
on Rue Lepsius, I sat at his desk
and imagined him there, entering
the study and seeing me.
"Young man," he said, though I was
no longer young, "not that I mind
your being here, but this room
is private." I looked out
the long window at the alley below,
then up over the rooftops of this
mythic Mediterranean city. It was
a rainy, windy December afternoon,
and here I sat in the poet's house.
"I didn't expect you," I replied.
"I was told that you were dead."
"Yes," he said, removing his hat
and coat, hanging them on a hook
on the back of the study door.
Cavafy moved toward me and stopped
on the other side of the desk.

"There used to be a brothel downstairs,
and around the corner Alexander the
Great's corpse lay in state, encased
in a gold sarcophagus."
Rain beat hard against the long window.
I could see tears starting from behind
Cavafy's glasses, then being absorbed
into his great mustache.
"When Forster was here," he said,
"staying at the Hotel Majestic, one evening
a boy came to his room, a very beautiful
boy, bearing a tea service. 'I knew
at once,' Forster told me, 'that his
was the face I had been expecting
all of my life.'"

Turning the Tightest Corner

for David Bromige

What do you think, David, now
that you've checked out
of this small hotel
into the Everlasting Arms?
You'd have a clever comeback
if you could make one, I know.
The night before you died
I had a dream—I was at a party,
people were talking and laughing
and you walked in, looking
as you had for most of the more
than forty-two years of our
friendship. You were smoking
a cigarette and chatting up
the prettiest girls. When I woke up
I knew it had been a premonition.
I was in New York and you were
in California and you'd come
to say goodbye the only way
you could. At your funeral
I recalled what your old
Winnipeg pal, Toby Oldfield,
used to say whenever you or he
hit a rough patch: It'll all
be all right in the end, Broms.
And I guess it is. The last
few years have been full of death.
I hate to admit it but it's that time

when friends and relatives start
dropping like flies. A dragonfly
lives three days, three short acts
to get everything done. It's probably
enough, and no great expectations.
That's the key, or one of them,
to not expect too much. Curiosity
may have killed the cat but it's
kept me going—it's the waning
of optimism that I fear.
How to stop it? This is
the tightest corner, David.
I hope we find each other again
among the majority to continue
our conversation. You can introduce me
to all the goodlooking girls
and show me around the enormous room.
I look forward to it.

Doggerel for
Barry McKinnon

Creeley really
taught you
what's taut
what
knot to
undo
what not

Certainly you
remember
the past
certainly

The New World

A few years ago I ran into an old girlfriend
in an expensive restaurant in Paris.
When I'd known her there, fifteen or more
years before, she was a slender, darkeyed,
darkhaired beauty recently arrived from Morocco.
Now she was fat, her breath stank of cheese,
and her hair was turning gray.
She was also more French than North African.
Gone were her large, clanging bracelets,
long, glittery earrings and colorful headwrap.
She told me she lived with an opera singer
in the eleventh arrondissement, and had long ago
given up her ambition to become a novelist.
I remembered her telling me how she and her mother
and her sisters would stand up to their hips
in the ocean and wash their clothes.
I remembered her whispering to me in Arabic
while we made love,
and that afterward she'd kiss me twice
on each of my eyes.
She'd had her chipped front tooth fixed.
What a pity, I said, I loved that tooth.

Paloma with Her Dogs

Here you are
not so long ago
sitting on front porch steps
pretty dress hiked up
so I can see your legs
caressing two dogs
with the same hands
since caressed
and handled me
Far away on a cold night
holding this photograph
like a kid
I need your heat, Paloma
or at least
two dogs

Begonia's Hands

Begonia's hands are huge.
Other than her hands
she is of average size for a woman of forty.
Her mouth is exotic
with full lips that curve down
slightly like Jeanne Moreau's,
and she has a good figure,
but it's her hands that are
her most notable feature.
She works as an upholsterer,
so her hands are very strong.
They recline in her lap,
palms up, like catchers' mitts.
The Boston Strangler must have
had hands like hers, or Poe's
villain in Murders in the Rue Morgue.
I can't take my eyes off of them.
I want Begonia to cradle my head
in those paws, knowing
she could crush the skull,
squeeze it as Astor Piazzolla
did his bandoneon, or Lenny
in Of Mice and Men mishandled
the rabbits and Curly's wife.
Staring at those big, rough fingers
I feel helpless, like Fay Wray
in Kong's grip. What could
be better?

Little Midnight Buddhist Poem

Don't take
your Self
so seriously
Remove the I
from I don't mind
you have
Don't mind
which, after
All, is all
you'll need
or ever
have

The Return

Last night or early this morning in a dream
I was visiting my mother at our old house
in Chicago, but it was not a house I recognized
as ever having lived in. She was in her forties,
I in my twenties. I heard her call my name
so I opened the door to my room, which was
next to the kitchen. A huge brown bull
with big yellow horns blocked my way—
the bull tried to get into the room
but I closed the door before he could.
I heard him clop away, then opened the door
a crack and shouted to my mother that she
should open the back door of the house so that
the bull could go out into the yard.
She came into the kitchen, her high heels
clacking against the linoleum, and stood
outside my room. I could hear people talking
and laughing, her party guests, in the front
of the house. Don't worry about the bull,
she said, he's used to company. The bull
trotted back into the kitchen, his hooves
scraping the floor like my mother's shoes.

I pushed past him, careful to avoid his
deadly headwear. My mother seemed not to mind
when he knocked down a table or dug a hole
in the wall with a horn. Aren't you afraid
the bull will gore you or your guests? I asked.
She was all dressed up, her hair piled high
like staggered amber bricks. Oh, no, she said,
flashing a red smile as she sipped a gooey liquid
from a martini glass. *El Chaparro* knows
just how far he can go with me.

Brain Damage

Thinking about Sugar Ray Robinson
        years past his prime
            at forty-four
    fighting in a dusty bullring
        in Tijuana, Mexico,
            losing a decision
        to a nobody
        named Memo Ayon
            who, after the fight,
            said to him,
                "Mister Ray, I sorry."
    Once you've been on top
        it's tough to quit,
            this we know
What we don't know
    is how to get
            these bad dreams
                to stop

Christmas Eve 2009

There are too many people
I can't call because
they're dead.
Listening to Monk play
Irving Berlin's "Remember"
it's too easy to imagine
them still there
at the other end
of the line, when
the end of the line
is where they are.
Now Monk's playing
"There's Danger in Your Eyes, Chérie"
As long as there's danger
in my eyes, there's hope.
Hello to all who can't answer.
I'll call back later, anyway.

New Year's Eve

I'm way out of touch.
I don't know the titles of hit songs
or the names of those who sing them.
I don't very often go to the movies.
As for current events,
weather reports are about it for me.
I'm the only person I know
who doesn't own a computer
or a cell phone.
I remember a kid I went to grammar school
with named Ronnie who flunked kindergarten
because he could not or would not
draw square windows in his pictures of houses.
The windows in his houses were always round.
When he was sixteen, Ronnie was killed
in a motorcycle accident.
I'm not missing anything.

BIBLIOGRAPHY

The Blood of the Parade published by A.G. Seepe at The Silverthorne Press, London, England, in 1967.

Coyote Tantras (Books I-IV) published by Melissa Mytinger at Christopher's Books, Santa Barbara, California, in 1973.

The Boy You Have Always Loved published by Dwight Gardiner at Talon Books, Vancouver, British Columbia, Canada in 1976.

Letters to Proust published by Dennis Maloney at White Pine Press, Buffalo, New York, in 1976.

Persimmons: Poems for Paintings published by Frederic Brunke at Shaman Drum, Berkeley, California, in 1977.

A Quinzaine in Return for a Portrait of Mary Sun published by Gary Wilkie at The Workingmans Press, Berkeley, California, and Seattle, Washington, in 1977.

Poems from Snail Hut published by Melissa Mytinger at Christopher's Books, Santa Barbara, California, in 1978.

Lives of the French Impressionist Painters published by Donald S. Ellis, Berkeley, California, in 1978.

Horse hauling timber out of Hokkaido forest published by Melissa Mytinger at Christopher's Books, Santa Barbara, California, in 1979.

Chinese Notes published by Donald S. Ellis, Berkeley, California, in 1980.

Beautiful Phantoms published by Michael Wolfe at Tombouctou Books, Bolinas, California, in 1981.

The Paris/Venice Poems published by Jim Haynes at Handshake Editions, Paris, France, in 1985.

Giotto's Circle published by David Rigsbee and Ronald Bayes at St. Andrews Press, Laurinburg, North Carolina, in 1987.

Ghosts No Horse Can Carry: Collected Poems 1967-1987 published by Creative Arts Book Company/Donald S. Ellis, Berkeley, California, in 1989.

Flaubert at Key West: New & Selected Poems 1967-1997 published by Lee Chapman at First Intensity Press, Lawrence, Kansas, in 1997.

Replies to Wang Wei published by Donald S. Ellis at Creative Arts Book Company, Berkeley, California, in 2001.

Back in America published by Joshua Clark at Light of New Orleans Press, New Orleans, Louisiana, in 2004.

Las cuatro reinas/The Four Queens published by Editorial Aldus, Mexico City, Mexico, in 2006. Bi-lingual edition. Spanish translation by Laura Emilia Pacheco.

Las cuatro reinas/The Four Queens published by La Fábrica Editorial, Madrid, Spain, in 2007. Bilingual edition with photographs by David Perry. Spanish translation by Laura Emilia Pacheco.

Back in America published by Renacimiento Editorial, Seville, Spain, in 2011. Bilingual edition. Spanish translation by Blanca Tortajada Perez.

"A black," 102
"A black and white cat," 89
"A few years ago I ran into an old girl-
friend," 335
"A friend once told me," 162
"A hundred and eleven," 27
"A monk sits mending," 127
"A puzzle," 199
"A room," 247
"A truck hauling a palm tree," 29
Adios, Chico!, 238
Afteft Selim, 327–328
After Listening to Bartók's From the
Diary of a Fly, 320
After Yosano Akiko, 51
"Ain't gettin," 249
Al Young's Blues, 319
"All of us," 243
"Along," 149
American Music, 232
April Again, 325
Art of Painting, The, 200
"As I told you," 207
At an Exhibition of Scrolls & Drawings
by Tomioka Tessai: 2nd December
1968," 58–63
At Apollinaire's Grave, Père-Lachaise,
89
At Bikky's Workshop, 172
At Ezra Pound's Grave, San Michele,
90
At Nishi-kokubunji, 175
"At Point Lobos," 13
"Ate, watered plants," 163
At the Albright-Knox, 43
"At the public bath," 174
"At the sorrow bar," 312
Autumn Landscape with Three Schol-
ars Enjoying Tea by a Stream, 140
"Awakened in Denver," 49
Axe, 134
"Azechi's fisherman," 156

"Back at my hut nobody bothers me,"
161
Back in America, 218
"Bad weather," 276

Bar Girls, 74
"Baudelaire died from," 297–298
"Baudelaire kept a Creole mistress," 81
"Beautiful girl," 73
"Beauty will drive," 203
Begonia's Hands, 337
"Begonia's hands are huge," 337
Bell Tower at Twilight, 143
"Big Dipper brow," 111
Blind Men Crossing a Bridge, 133
Blonde Light, 98
Boat on a Windy Sea, 142
Boca Chica, 214
Bodhidharma, 111
Bohemian Cigar Store, San Francisco,
46
Bordertown, 226-229
"Bordertown," 226
Brain Damage, 341
Brigands, 210
Buddhist Poem, 178
Building a House in the Mountains, 153

"Callejon de los Manzanares," 269
Change in the Weather, 235
"Charles, from the beginning you al-
ways," 84
Chinatown Carnival Night, 234
"Chinese children chase pigeons," 40
"Chinese flew to Mexico," 264
Chinese Note for Mary Lou, A, 100
Chinese Notes, 64–71
"'Chopping word,'" 134
Christ in the House of Martha and
Mary, 189
Christmas Eve 2009, 342
Cino, 45
Claire Bloom's Face, 78
Clear Morning in a Mountain Village,
123
"Climbing all those," 320
Cocteau's Hands, 309
"Combing snowflakes," 105
"Come into this dream," 314
"Come on, Al, you," 319
"Coming from your bed," 51
Concert, The, 198

Cormorant Fisherman, 157
"Coyote did not know how to swim," 16
"Coyote sat," 19
"Coyote stood by the river," 18
Coyote Tantras XV, 13
Coyote Tantras XXXVII, 14–15
Coyote Tantras LXXXVIII, 16
Coyote Tantras XCIX, 17
Coyote Tantras CI, 18
Coyote Tantras CII, 19
Coyote Tantras CXVI, 20
Coyote Tantras CXVII, 21
"Coyote traversed," 20
"Cranes slowly," 101
"Creek," 221
"Creeley really," 334
"Crossing," 170
Crow in a Wintry Sky, A, 147
Crows Taking Flight Through Spring
    Haze, 151
"Cruising in a Cadillac," 86

"'Dancing' Taoist," 112
Day Allen Ginsberg Died, The, 222
"Dear M.," 47
"Dear Marcel," 48
Delacroix's Atelier, Late October, 88
"Delacroix's painting, 'Coin," 88
Denver Alba, 49
Devil or Angel, 324
Diana and Her Companions, 188
"Do it again," 281
Doggerel for Barry McKinnon, 334
"Don't eat," 280
"Don't look like," 262
"Don't take," 338
Dream, A, 207–208
"Dreaming I'm an eagle," 164
"Dusk, Oakland—," 232

Epiphany for Gérald Neveu, 29
Eurydice in Romania, 239
"Evening haze," 120
"Exhausted by understanding," 131

Faded Love, 313
"Falling out of love," 75
Farewell Letter from Jeanne Duval to
    Charles Baudelaire, 84–85
Few Words about Rimbaud, A, 27–28

Fifth Patriarch Planting Pine Trees,
    The, 145
Fishermen on the Great River," 150
Flaubert at Key West, 95
"Fleas are my worst enemy," 162
"Fog surrounds the mountains," 129
"Fogborne bands," 123
"Following fog," 151
For My Winnie at The Negresco, 93
"For years I was lost," 235
"Forged on flowers," 80
"Friedrich Nietzsche used to walk," 306
"From a Gamalia alley," 327
"Fruit trees, flowers," 155
Furo-ya, 174

Genealogy, 329
Generalissimo Waves, The, 301–302
Giotto's Circle, 92
Girl Asleep at a Table, 187
Girl with a Pearl Earring, 199
Glass of Wine, The, 192
Going to Meet Mike, 315
"Gorgeous Gypsy girl, perhaps," 239
"Great Waves," 126
"Gregory Corso's buried in Rome," 220
"Groping, hoping," 133
"Gyokudō," 152

Haboku Landscape, 129
"Han Shan," 158
Han Shan and Shih-te, 159
"Happen right here," 287
"Having one's feet washed," 188
"He pours," 192
"Hello, Bees," 316
"Her eyes were like," 261
"Her name," 255
"Her self-fascination," 195
"Here on the mountain," 169
"Here you are," 336
Hey, Ludwig, Grab Yourself a Pigfoot,
    311
"Hey Pete," 248
"Hidalgo goes every day," 271
"Hiding his head," 124
Highway 83, 31
"Hiking back toward," 143
"Holding the pitcher," 185
Horse hauling timber out of Hokkaido
    forest, 167

"Horses slip," 148
Hotei in a Boat, 137
"Hotei in a boat," 137
"How could I know," 288
"How crow," 147
How Many Mangos in Mango Chutney, 37
"Hui-k'o came to see Bodhidharma," 115
Hui-k'o Cutting Off His Arm, 115
"Hui-neng kneels," 122
"Hung-jen," 145
"Hunter in the Kootenays," 17

"I," 103
"I am no painter," 173
"I am surrounded by death," 313
"I ask her," 256
"I begin," 108
"I call this place 'Snail Hut' like Chao-Hsien's," 162
"I'd be confined," 233
"I'd rather be alone here than anywhere," 165
"I did for," 286
"I don't go anywhere," 277
"I don't know if you remember me," 209
"I got almost," 279
"I got up early," 222
"I had a visitation last night," 307
"I have a friend," 72
"I keep," 107
"I kill," 267
"I like you," 253
"I love these," 237
"I love to listen to Monk," 231
"I miss seeing the magnolia," 217
"I only saw the Colosseum," 305
"I recall your," 109
"I remember the exact moment," 326
"I remembered Veracruz," 294
"I used to have," 273
"If often I appear righteous," 162
"If you don't," 283
"I'm way out of touch," 343
"Imagine lying in bed," 212
"In 1959, my cousin Chris and I," 22
"In 1975, I went to Japan," 303
"In Alexandria, in Cavafy's apartment," 330
"In Barcelona," 25
"In Iwatsuki," 179

"In Madrid," 325
In Memory of Suwa Yu, 221
"In Mexico some people," 268
In Sight, 36
"In sleep," 132
"In the Cuban night," 213
"In the Egyptian," 329
"In the end," 293
"In Zapata, Texas," 31
"It got broke," 259
"It is because we die," 196
"It was all a long time ago," 214
"It's pouring now," 321
"It's sooner," 246
"It's terrible," 204

Japan North: Two Paintings, 156
"Just off train," 315

Kannon, 118
"Kannon's face," 118
"Kao's cormorant," 157
"Kick it again," 282
"Kid Gavilian is dead," 238

Lady Holding Fan, 160
Lady with Her Maidservant, 202
Lady Writing a Letter, 201
Landscape at Lushan, 126
Landscape with Traveler and Woodgatherer, 139
Landscape with Travelers, 141
Larry, 38
"Last night or early this morning in a dream," 339
"Last night there was," 323
"Last week," 46
"Late at night I lie alone," 165
"Late autumn," 205
Late September in Toronto and the Weather is Still Fair, 237
"Laughing and pointing," 159
Letter from La Habana, 212
Letter to Proust No. 2, 47
Letter to Proust No. 5, 48
Life & Death with an Actress, 211
"Li-Po and Coyote lay drunk," 21
Li-Po Reciting Verse, 121
Life of Wang Wei by Chang Chiu-ling, The, 103–110
"Listening to Noche de Biarritz," 301

"Listening to the Clovers sing," 324
Little Midnight Buddhist Poem, 338
Little Street, The, 193
Lives of the French Impressionist
    Painters, 52–57
"Living with you," 215
"logging done in winter," 167
Looking for Nanao, 303–304
"Lonely for conversation," 116
"Lorca at the," 26
"Lying in state, under glass," 219

"Man and horse," 141
"Man don'," 290
"Man Ray's photograph," 83
Man with an Ox, 117
Maracas, 26
Maria La O, 22–23
Memento, 217
Milkmaid, The, 185
"Missing you," 93
"Mist rising over Northern Honshu,"
    176
Moment of Enlightenment, The, 135
"Monet had a beautiful garden that," 52
Monk Gazing at a Waterfall, 113
Monk in the Morning, 231
"Monk's 'Functional' (1956)," 311
Monk's Funeral, 299–300
Morning at Mt. Yatsu, 171
Morning Sun at Uji, 154
"Murderous dogs," 107
"Music, companion of," 197
Music Lesson, The, 197
Música Latina, 25
"My arm," 50
My Father, 35
"My father rode with," 275
My Last Sonnet, 209
"My mother," 38
"My mother's name," 278
Myna Bird on a Pine Tree, 124
Myriad Sounds and Thousand-layered
    Peaks, A, 152

Nan-ch'uan Chopping the Kitten in
    Two, 146
"Native of," 104
New Moon Over the Brushwood Gate,
    136
New World, The, 335

New Year's Eve, 343
New York Movie, 79
Night Train to Mt. Yatsu, 168
Nine May Ninety-six, 24
"No ocean," 153
"Nobody told me," 285
North Beach Chinese Sonnet, 40
North of Tokyo, 176
Note on Inspiration for Duane Big
    Eagle, A, 81
Note to a Friend Far Away, 101
"Note to Winter Guests," 163
"Now there's a man," 263
Nudes, 83
Nunobukuro, 132

"O beauties," 45
"O fly," 76
"O silent love," 44
"Of course, Jammes was mad," 30
Officer with a Laughing Girl, 191
"Oh baby," 245
Old Boy, The, 10–12
"Old cowboy," 218
"Old man," 32
"Old Tessai," 58
"On a wood bench," 178
"On my door I've tacked a painting," 161
On Viewing the Manuscript Scroll of
    Jack Kerouac's Novel On the Road in
    the Tosca Bar, San Francisco, 219
"Only one pays," 194
Orchids and Bamboo Beneath the
    Moon, 128
"Orchids, bamboo," 128
Owl on a Bare Tree, 130

"Paco tell you," 292
"Paddling past," 154
"Paloma gave it," 274
Paloma with Her Dogs, 336
Paris Street, 39
"Pascin knew something about beauty,"
    82
"Past midnight at her loom," 163
"Perhaps she's," 187
Persimmons, 119
Phoebe's Profile, 80
"Place: The Hospital of the Immaculate
    Conception," 180
"Plea to Coyote For Mankind," 14

Poem, 9, 50, 75, 102, 173, 179, 204, 206, 310
Poem (1978), 312
Poem for a Painter, 72
Poem for Pascin, 82
Poem in the Style of Wang Wei, 177
Poem Ut Animum Nostrum Purget, 34
Poet at the Hôtel Sordide, The, 297–298
Poet's House, The, 330–331
"Pollock's painting," 43
Procuress, The, 190
Pseudo-Pindaric Ode to Francis
    Jammes, 30
Pu-tai, 112

Rabbit and Moon, 138
"Radio Havana still plays," 47
"Rain splinters the bridge," 36
"Raindrops from," 109
Rainy Tijuana, 230
Reading in the Study in the Bamboo
    Grove, 116
"Red and gold surround," 189
Redux, 91
Remember, It's Only a Movie, 317
"Remember when," 260
"Remembering bum outskirts of
    Tokyo," 164
Return, The, 339–340
Returning by Boat on a Cold River, 149
"Riding slow in taxi," 230
Rising Sun Sonnet, 169
Road to Shu, The, 148
"Rodolfo Fierro," 252
Rue des Abbesses, 203

Sākyamuni Descending the Mountain,
    131
Season of Truth, The, 42
Second Patriarch Setting His Mind in
    Order, The, 125
"Seeing again," 317
"Separated by a river," 64
September 11, 2001, 236
Shanghai Garden, 233
"She is pregnant," 184
"She lov'd Villon—," 34
Shooting Pool in the Dark, 215
"Silence, silence," 9
"Sitting alone," 10

Sitting on the Porch Swing Imagining
    Paradise I Am Embraced By My
    Old Sweetheart, Emily Dickinson,
    Who, Among Other Things, In-
    forms Me That She Has Missed
    Me Greatly, 316
"Sitting still, lilacs," 164
"Six Persimmons—," 119
Sixth Patriarch Cutting Bamboo, The,
    122
Sleepy Time Down South, 94
"Slender lady," 160
Small Elegy for Corso, 220
"Snowy February day in New York
    1982," 299
"So," 309
"So complicated," 110
"So many men," 150
"So often full of bitterness," 165
"Somewhere up," 284
Song, 76
Sonnet to a Marble Beauty, 44
"Sounds of," 106
Southern Air, 96
Sunrise, 127
Sunset in a Fishing Village, 120
Surrealists Come to California, The,
    86–87
Swallows, 144
"swoop," 144

"Talking in the blowing grass,—," 140
"Teresa this is the last," 242
Thank You Note to Chekhov, A, 326
"That old DelRay," 291
"That road broke," 254
"That the thought," 206
"The battered seacoast captain," 142
"The chicken his name," 266
"The Chinese," 236
"The clouds," 135
"The day," 35
"The farmer's foot," 117
"The Florida sky unwraps," 96
"The founder of Zen," 125
"The Japanese brakeman," 168
"The maid delivers," 202
"The matador Luis Miguel Domin-
    guín," 24
"The moon," 138
"The other night," 92

"The pain in my heart does not stop,"
    177
"The sound of," 99
"The topographical map of Holland,"
    191
"The waterfall," 113
"The way the land dips," 114
"There are too many people," 342
"There is a broken heart," 37
"There she is," 241
"There you are in 1939," 79
"Thick black branch," 130
Thief's World, The, 305
"Thinking about Sugar Ray Robinson,"
    341
"This backyard," 100
"This is the Day of the Dead," 90
"This is valuable experience," 42
"This morning I am not," 77
"This woman," 201
Tiger, The, 323
To Terry Moore, 77
"Tonight shat in the rain," 165
Toward Dusk, 170
Travel Sketches of Konodai, 155
Traveling Light, 99
Tropical Street, 97
True Love, 216
Turning the Tightest Corner, 332–333
Tuscany, 318
Twelfth Street, 73
Two Landscapes, 114

Übermensch, 306
"Under dim," 33
"Under waving palms," 95
"Unlike the milkmaid," 186
Unsent Letter from La Habana, 213
"Using gempitsu," 121

"Vermeer and his friends," 190
View of Rain in the Tropics, 321–322
Vision del Calle Cruz Rey, 32
Visit, The, 307–308

"Walking in Kensington Gardens," 91
"Warm tears," 108
"Watching," 41
Watching Fish, 41
"We preserve," 265
"We see the beginnings," 198

"We were at the Antinori castle," 318
"What do you think, David, now," 332
"What doesn't have meaning," 146
"What if a big," 272
"What is," 310
"What peace sleeps," 136
"What the church," 244
"What would these girls," 74
"What you doing," 257
"When Estrellita," 250
"When I was away," 163
"When I was five," 78
"Who holds," 240
Whores in the Club Papagayo, 33
"Why are Clio's," 200
"Why there gotta be," 289
"Why you want to," 258
"Wind up gray," 39
"Without lost steps," 139
"Without you," 166
"Wizened Chinese bum," 234
Woman and Two Men, 194
Woman in Blue Reading a Letter, 184
Woman Weighing Gold, 196
Woman with a Pearl Necklace, 195
Woman with a Water Jug, 186
"Women and children," 193
"Woodchips strewn," 172
"Woodpecker woke me—," 171
"Worst things that can happen," 161

"You came to me last night," 94
"You can," 251
"You used to come down the stone
    path," 164
Young Girl's Crime, The, 314
"Young Japanese girl," 175
"Your dream of Sardinia—, 210
Your Face, 205
"Your idea," 211
"Your scent still," 98
"Your sickness made me," 216

Zen Poet Han Shan, 158

ABOUT BARRY GIFFORD

Barry Gifford's fiction, nonfiction, and poetry have been published in twenty-eight languages. His novel *Night People* was awarded the Premio Brancati, established by Pier Paolo Pasolini and Alberto Moravia, in Italy, and he has been the recipient of awards from PEN, the National Endowment for the Arts, the American Library Association, the Writers Guild of America, and the Christopher Isherwood Foundation. His books *Sailor's Holiday* and *The Phantom Father* were each named a Notable Book of the Year by the *New York Times*, and his book *Wyoming* was named a Novel of the Year by the *Los Angeles Times*. He has written librettos for operas by the composers Toru Takemitsu, Ichiro Nodaira, and Olga Neuwirth. Gifford's work has appeared in many publications, including the *The New Yorker*, *Punch*, *Esquire*, *La Nouvelle Revue Française*, *El País*, *La Repubblica*, *Rolling Stone*, *Brick*, *Film Comment*, *El Universal*, *Projections*, and the *New York Times*. His film credits include *Wild at Heart*, *Perdita Durango*, *Lost Highway*, *City of Ghosts*, *Ball Lightning*, and *The Phantom Father*. Barry Gifford's most recent books are *Sailor & Lula: The Complete Novels* and *Sad Stories of the Death of Kings*. He lives in the San Francisco Bay Area. For more information, visit www.BarryGifford.com.